Care of Sick Children

A Basic Guide

Other titles by Ausmed Publications

Gynaecological Cancer Care: A Guide to Practice
Edited by Tish Lancaster and Kathryn Nattress
Available as audiobook and textbook

Wound Care Nursing: A Guide to Practice
Edited by Sue Templeton
Available as audiobook and textbook

Gastrostomy Care: A Guide to Practice
Edited by Catherine Barrett
Available as audiobook and textbook

Nursing Documentation in Aged Care: A Guide to Practice
Edited by Christine Crofton and Gaye Witney
Available as audiobook and textbook

Nurse Managers: A Guide to Practice
Edited by Andrew Crowther
Available as audiobook and textbook

Aged Care Nursing: A Guide to Practice
Edited by Susan Carmody and Sue Forster
Available as audiobook and textbook

Dementia Nursing: A Guide to Practice
Edited by Rosalie Hudson
Available as audiobook and textbook

Palliative Care Nursing: A Guide to Practice (2nd edn)
Edited by Margaret O'Connor and Sanchia Aranda

Lymphoedema
Edited by Robert Twycross, Karen Jenns, and Jacquelyne Todd

Communicating with Dying People and their Relatives
Jean Lugton

How Drugs Work
Hugh McGavock

Evidence-based Management
Rosemary Stewart

Communication and the Manager's Job
Annie Phillips

Assertiveness and the Manager's Job
Annie Phillips

Renal Nursing--A Practical Approach
Bobbee Terrill

Ageing at Home--Practical Approaches to Community Care
Edited by Theresa Cluning

Complementary Therapies in Nursing and Midwifery
Edited by Pauline McCabe

Keeping in Touch--with someone who has Alzheimer's
Jane Crisp

Geriatric Medicine--a pocket guide for doctors, nurses, other health professionals and students (2nd edn)
Len Gray, Michael Woodward, Ron Scholes, David Fonda & Wendy Busby

Living Dying Caring--life and death in a nursing home
Rosalie Hudson & Jennifer Richmond

Caring for People with Problem Behaviours (2nd edn)
Bernadette Keane & Carolyn Dixon

Practical Approaches to Infection Control in Residential Aged Care (2nd edn)
Kevin Kendall

All of these titles are available from the publisher:
Ausmed Publications
277 Mt Alexander Road, Ascot Vale, Melbourne, Victoria 3032, Australia
website: <www.ausmed.com.au>
email: <ausmed@ausmed.com.au>

Care of Sick Children
A Basic Guide

Gerry Silk

Ausmed Publications
Melbourne – Seattle

Ausmed Publications Pty Ltd
Melbourne – Seattle

Melbourne office:
277 Mt Alexander Road
Ascot Vale, Melbourne, Victoria 3032, Australia
ABN 49 824 739 129
Telephone: + 61 3 9375 7311
Fax: + 61 3 9375 7299
email: <ausmed@ausmed.com.au>
website: <www.ausmed.com.au>

Seattle office:
Martin P. Hill Consulting
157 Yesler Way, Suite 300
Seattle, Washington 98104
USA
Tel: 206-624-6609
Fax: 206-624-6707
Mobile: 415-309-2338
email: <mphill@mphconsult.com>

Care of Sick Children: A Basic Guide
ISBN (13-digit): 978-0-9752018-3-1
ISBN (10-digit): 0-9752018-3-2

First published by Ausmed Publications Pty Ltd, 2006.

National Library of Australia Cataloguing-in-Publication data

Silk, Geraldine Barbara.
Care of sick children : a basic guide.
Bibliography.
Includes index.
ISBN 0 9752018 3 2.
ISBN 0 9752018 4 0 (CD: not sold separately).
ISBN 0 9752018 5 9 (Book + CD).
1. Sick children - Care. 2. Children - Health and hygiene -
Handbooks, manuals, etc. 3. Child care - Handbooks, manuals, etc. I. Title.

649.8

Produced by Ginross Publishing <www.ginross.com.au>

Printed in China

Contents

Introduction

Care of Sick Children: A Basic Guide is written for all those parents and carers who have felt the anxiety of not knowing what they should do when a previously well child in their care is suddenly injured or unexpectedly becomes unwell. Caring for a sick or injured child can be a frightening experience—especially for parents and carers who have not previously dealt with the medical problem that suddenly confronts them. Even those with the advantage of previous experience or formal medical/nursing training can become alarmed. Children tend to get sick quickly, and although they also usually get better relatively quickly, parents and carers can be understandably worried if they do not know what to do. This book aims to provide the basic knowledge and skills needed to cope with these potentially alarming situations.

This book aims to provide the basic knowledge and skills needed to cope with these potentially alarming situations.

The idea for this book came from the interest shown in seminar/conferences that I have been conducting for Ausmed for a number of years. These seminars are entitled 'Basic Care of Sick Children', and they aim to cover the 'basics' of what carers need to know about illness and injury in the children for whom they are responsible. The people attending these conferences come from an astonishing range of backgrounds and occupations—including teachers, childcare staff, first-aid officers, receptionists in clinics, sick bay attendants, parents, and so on. Many of these people have had little or no formal medical/nursing training, although a number of trained nurses come along to refresh their knowledge and skills.

The seminars have been very successful and popular. Those who attend the seminars consistently say how helpful they have been in giving them essential information about the care of sick children. More importantly, many report how they have gained in confidence in their various roles as carers of children. As a result of the success and popularity of these seminars, Ausmed Publications saw the potential for bringing this vital information to a wider audience through a book.

Many report how they have gained in confidence in their various roles as carers of children.

The original idea was simply to 'make the book like the seminars'—by recording a seminar and putting the words on paper. However, it soon became apparent that this wouldn't work—because a book and a seminar are quite different things. In particular, a seminar allows for mutual interaction and feedback, but a book does not. For example, in a seminar it is possible for people in the audience to ask questions or seek clarification if they are unsure of what has been said. This is obviously impossible when reading a book! And in a seminar the presenter can get a 'feel' for the audience, and can make adjustments in the presentation to fit in with the audience's level of understanding and degree of interest. For example, depending on the reaction of the audience, the presenter can rearrange the order of topics (and the amount of time taken on each one), change the language and terminology that is used, give more examples to clarify certain points, and generally respond to the needs of listeners. This sort of positive mutual interaction between presenter and audience goes on all the time in a seminar, but is simply not possible in writing and reading a book. What's written is written, and readers can't chat with authors about their queries!

All readers, no matter what their professional background, can pick up this book with confidence.

So in producing this book, it soon became apparent that this was not as simple as recording a seminar and then printing the words in a book. It was necessary to make careful decisions about the style and content of the book.

With regard to *style*, we wanted to make the book accessible to as wide an audience as possible. It was therefore decided that it was best to assume that readers had no prior training in medicine, nursing, or first aid. Technical jargon has therefore been deliberately kept to a minimum, and when a few 'technical' terms *are* used here and there, these are explained in handy 'Boxes' in the text. There is also a full glossary of these terms at the back of the book. By assuming that readers have no formal medical/nursing training, and by keeping technical language to a minimum, it is hoped that all readers, no matter what their professional background, can pick up this book with confidence, knowing that they will be able to follow what is being said.

With regard to *content*, the problem was deciding what to put in and what to leave out. There are many illnesses and injuries that *could* be included in a book such as this, but we didn't want to turn it into a huge encyclopaedia of every possible childhood disease, and how doctors and nurses treat them all. It was therefore decided that the book should be a 'basic guide' to childhood medical problems that are either *common* or *important.* In saying that the book is a 'basic guide', the word 'basic' is used to mean 'fundamental' or 'essential'—rather than 'basic' meaning 'simplistic' or 'superficial'. The book therefore provides essential information on the fundamental care of most of the important problems that might confront parents and carers in looking after children. There is some information on what doctors and nurses do, and on what happens in hospitals, but the focus of the book is on what parents and carers should do in the 'basic' (or *fundamental* and *essential*) care of sick children.

The book provides essential information on the fundamental care of most of the important problems that might confront parents and carers in looking after children.

The book can be read from cover to cover, or specific chapters and sections of the text can be read as required. If parents and carers want to look up a specific problem, they will find that the table of contents is quite detailed and useful. It not only provides a list of the titles of the chapters, but also provides a guide to the subheadings within each chapter. If readers cannot find what they are looking for from the table of contents, the index at the back of the book should be consulted. This contains an alphabetical list (and page numbers) of all the main topics covered in the book.

I trust that parents and carers find the book to be useful and enlightening. More importantly, I trust that it gives them greater confidence in undertaking their crucial role as carers of children. If the parents and carers who read this book gain in knowledge and confidence, and if the children they look after receive better care and attention, the book will have achieved its purpose.

If parents and carers gain in knowledge and confidence, and if children receive better care and attention, the book will have achieved its purpose.

Gerry Silk
February 2006

Chapter 1

What's Different about Children?

Little adults?

Children are often thought of as 'little adults', but they are anatomically, physiologically, and psychologically different. The tendency of some people to think of children as 'little adults' was humorously highlighted in a satirical 'medical report' that discussed childhood as though it were a disease![1] In this 'report', children were supposed to have a number of specific signs and symptoms of 'disease'. These so-called signs and symptoms of 'disease' included:

- a congenital onset (the 'disease' of childhood always seems to begin at birth!);
- dwarfism (children are smaller than adult people!);
- emotional immaturity (children are less mature than adult people!);
- significant knowledge deficits (children do not know as much about the world as adult people!); and
- legume anorexia (children often have a lack of appetite when it comes to eating green vegetables!).

Apparently most children recover from this 'disease' without any specific treatment!

The point of this satirical 'medical report' was to highlight, in a humorous way, that it is silly to think of children as being adults with a 'disease'—or to think of them as being just 'little adults'.

Children *are* different. They are different from adults in their anatomy, their physiology, and their psychology.

Children *are* different. They are different from adults in their anatomy, their physiology, and their psychology. Most children are healthy to start with—although some are born with congenital diseases. As healthy children grow older, illnesses, injuries, and the ageing process damage their bodies. Various problems begin to emerge—including heart disease, respiratory problems, and so on.

Physical and physiological differences

Airways

Children are obviously smaller than adults. One of the most important physical differences is the size of the airways (the tubes leading to the lungs). The size of the trachea (the 'windpipe') in an adult is surprisingly small; it is only 8–10 millimetres in diameter—which is about the size of an adult's little finger. In a 12-month-old child, the trachea is only about 4 millimetres in diameter. This means that even the largest airway is very narrow indeed. The trachea then divides into smaller and smaller airways (the bronchi and bronchioles) to pass air into the lungs.

The small size of the airways in children (especially young children) means that they are very prone to obstruction from even small objects or minimal swelling.

The small size of the airways in children (especially young children) means that they are very prone to obstruction from even small objects or minimal swelling. This is why children can quickly become distressed from infections such as croup. And this is why their airways can be blocked if they inhale small foreign objects—such as peanuts or parts of plastic toys.

Pulse rate and respiratory rate

Children have higher pulse rates and breathing rates than adults. Their metabolic rates are higher, and they need to transport oxygen and nutrients around the body more quickly. Normal pulse rates and breathing rates are shown in the Box below.

Pulse rates and breathing rates

Pulse rates and breathing rates are higher in children than in adults.

Pulse rates

Normal pulse rates are as follows:

- *newborn infants:* 100–160 beats per minute
- *children 1–10 years:* 70–120 beats per minute
- *children more than 10 years and adults:* 60–100 beats per minute

Breathing rates

Normal respiratory rates are as follows:

- *newborn infants:* 30–60 breaths per minute
- *early childhood:* 20–40 breaths per minute
- *late childhood and adulthood:* 15–25 breaths per minute

Fluid balance

Children lose fluid more quickly than adults—and can therefore become dehydrated more rapidly.

The small intestine of small children is comparatively much longer than an adult's small intestine. Children can therefore lose fluid from the bowel much more quickly than adults.

The length of an adult's small intestine is about four times the adult's height. For example, an adult who is 2 metres tall has a small intestine that is approximately 8 metres long. In contrast, a small child's intestine is *six times* the child's height. This means that a child with gastroenteritis can lose relatively much more fluid from the intestine than an adult will lose. A small child with gastroenteritis is therefore much more likely to become dangerously dehydrated—and this can happen relatively quickly compared with an adult.

The kidneys of children are relatively immature compared with adults. The kidneys of a child do not respond to external conditions as efficiently as an adult. For example, on a hot day, adults will pass less urine because their kidneys retain fluid by reabsorbing it and not passing it from the body. In contrast, the kidneys of small children continue to pass urine freely. They are therefore more likely to become dehydrated in hot weather. Every hour, an adult passes approximately half a millilitre of fluid for every kilogram of body weight. In contrast, every hour a baby passes approximately *two* millilitres of urine per kilogram of body weight. This is *four times* as great! This is why it is important to ask whether small children are having wet nappies (diapers). If not, the child is likely to be dehydrated—if they could pass urine, they would!

Immunity

When babies are born, they have some degree of immunity from the mother. This is increased if babies are then breastfed. However, this immunity then begins to wear off. At five months of age, their immunity is at its lowest. Then they begin to get infections—and build up their immunity as a result. By the age of four years, most children have attained quite good levels of immunity.

Between the ages of one year and five years, an average child will have about 8–10 infections per year—more if they are in child care. This is not necessarily a bad thing—if they do not contract these diseases during their early years, their immunity will be underdeveloped.

Between the ages of one year and five years, an average child will have about 8–10 infections per year—more if they are in child care.

Assessing a sick child

Beware the quiet child!

When dealing with children, a good 'rule of thumb' for carers to follow is: 'Beware the quiet child!'. Carers are understandably alarmed if a child is screaming and making a lot of noise. And it is true that such a child might be in pain. However, this is not likely to be life-threatening. Children who are unusually quiet are the ones to be worried about! These children are more likely to be very sick. These are the children who require immediate attention.

Who is with the child?

Children rarely come alone to a healthcare clinic or sick bay. In most cases a parent, carer, or friend accompanies the child.

This person will know more about the child than whoever is providing the health care. He or she can therefore provide a lot of useful information. However, the accompanying person is also likely to be worried about the child; indeed, the carer (especially a parent) might be more worried about the illness than the child is!

It is very important to reassure the person who is accompanying the child. A worried parent means a worried child. Ensuring that the parent is relaxed will be a great help in interactions with the sick child. A relaxed parent or other carer is also more likely to be able to supply useful information about the illness in a calm manner.

Initial impressions are important

In assessing young children, initial impressions are important. In fact, such general impressions are usually more important than measuring vital signs (such as temperature and pulse). Intuition and first impressions usually provide more valuable information than counting a pulse or breathing rate.

Small children are genuine

Small children (younger than school age) are genuine. Pre-school children are very unlikely to say that they have pain if they do not really have pain. They are very unlikely to 'fake' a limp. If they look worried, they *are* worried. If they act sick (or say that they are sick)—they *are* sick!

> If small children look worried, they *are* worried. If they act sick, they *are* sick!

In addition, pre-school children are very unlikely to 'cover up' illness or pain. Older children might deny that they have pain because they are aware that they might receive unwanted medical attention—such as an injection. In contrast, younger (pre-school) children are not aware of consequences, and are therefore likely to give an honest account of their symptoms.

Communicating with children

Choosing the right words

Children are not only physically different from adults—they also think differently. Carers need to explain to children what is happening to them in terms that children will understand.

A lot of the language that is used in medical and nursing settings can be confusing to children. For example, terms such as 'trolley' and 'dressing' are easily understood by adults and health professionals. But, for a child, a 'trolley' is something that is pushed around a supermarket, and a 'dressing' sounds like clothing worn by girls! Carers should therefore be careful to use words that children will understand—such as 'bandage' or 'band-aid' (rather than 'dressing'). If a child needs stitches, it is better to talk about 'cotton' or 'string'—rather than 'sutures'.

Imagination often worse than reality

Imagination is often worse than reality for sick or injured children. Carers should be aware that a child's imagination can often make things seem to be much worse than they really are. Carers should always explain and demonstrate what is happening and what is about to be done. If children know what to expect, they are much more likely to relax.

Cuts and bleeding are especially likely to cause anxiety. For example, if a child has a cut that is bleeding, he or she will often fear the worst—even if the cut is relatively minor in itself. A laceration to the scalp is a good example of a wound that bleeds profusely, but is often relatively minor. The best thing to do is to demonstrate to the child that everything is under control, and that the wound is not dangerous. Carers should reassure the child that everything is going to be all right, clean the wound, stop the bleeding, and show the small wound to the child (with a mirror if necessary). Children will become much more relaxed if they can see that cuts are not life-threatening.

Familiar people (such as parents or friends) can help with reassurance and assistance in minor procedures—such as removing clothing or bathing.

Children often feel more vulnerable and intimidated if they are forced to lie down—especially in an unfamiliar environment. Allowing (or encouraging) a child to sit up can remove anxiety because it removes a sense of powerlessness.

Allowing a child to sit up can remove anxiety because it removes a sense of powerlessness.

Using calico dolls as 'models' can help to reassure small children. Children will often transfer their anxieties to a doll if carers encourage children to perceive the doll as having an injury or an illness.

The story of 'Peter' (Box, below) illustrates how sensitive carers can help to alleviate anxiety by reassuring children and helping them to understand what is going on.

Peter

Peter was a five-year-old boy who had been taken to a hospital with burns to his feet. A nurse heard Peter screaming with pain and anxiety, and went to investigate.

She discovered that Peter had been placed on his back on a trolley behind some curtains. Although his mother was in attendance, the little boy was terrified in this intimidating, strange environment.

The nurse immediately arranged for Peter to sit up with his injured feet over the side of the trolley. The little boy was reassured, and his mother was encouraged to bathe his feet gently before dressings were applied.

Peter was given a calico doll to hold. As Peter's burns were being dressed, the doll's 'burns' were also dressed. Peter was encouraged to do his own drawing of the doll's burns and treatment.

In a very short time, Peter's anxiety disappeared. Indeed, he was transformed. He was no longer screaming and anxious. He became cooperative and chatty—happily describing how his doll's 'burns' had been fixed up by being bathed and dressed.

Response to illness and treatment

It is important for carers to remember that children become sick very quickly—but they get better very quickly too! It is true that carers must be alert for signs and symptoms which indicate that a child is becoming unwell. However, carers should also be aware that children recover more quickly than adults—and this is one of the joys of caring for sick children.

Note

1. This humorous article appeared as a formal 'academic paper' by Jordan W. Smoller of the University of Pennyslvania. It was intended as satire. It is available on various websites on the Internet, including <www.pfc.org.uk/satire/smoller.htm>.

Chapter 2

Fevers and Febrile Convulsions

What is a fever?

Fevers are common in young children. In fact, having a fever is one of the most common reasons for children being taken to a doctor or hospital emergency department.

What is a fever? A fever can be defined as *a centrally regulated rise in temperature in response to some pathological stimulus.* In simple terms, something has gone wrong (such as an infection) and this has caused the body to raise its temperature.

Framework of chapter

This chapter discusses the basic care of children with a fever. The chapter discusses the following subjects:

It is difficult to be precise about how high a child's temperature has to be to constitute a 'fever'. Although it is generally assumed that 'normal' temperature is 36.9 degrees Celsius (°C), a healthy person's temperature actually changes during the course of the day. In fact, about 50% of healthy 18-month-old children have a temperature of 38°C by 6 pm in the evening. Children have a high metabolic rate, and their temperatures rise by at least half a degree during the day, even if they sit down and do nothing. And if they are running around with a high metabolic rate, the temperature rises even more.

Parents should not panic if a child is found to have a temperature of 38°C in the evening after having run around during the day.

So parents should not panic if a child is found to have a temperature of 38°C in the evening after having run around during the day. On the other hand, if a child had a temperature of 38.5°C first thing in the morning, this might would be a greater cause for concern than a similar temperature in an active child at the end of the day.

Despite the fact that normal temperatures can vary quite widely, there are some broad guidelines for what constitutes a 'fever'. The Box below provides a useful guide.

Guidelines for a fever

Although normal temperature varies, the following temperatures provide useful guidelines for judging whether a child's temperature constitutes a fever.

Oral (in the mouth)
Above about 37.6°C (or perhaps 38°C)

Rectal
Above about 38°C

Aural (ear probes)
Above about 38°C

Axilla (under the arm)
Above about 37.5°C

Assessing sick children with a fever

Taking a child's temperature can be difficult—and is usually unnecessary. It is much more important to assess the overall condition of the child. A child can have a 'high fever' but remain generally quite well. In contrast, a child can have a 'low fever' (or even a 'normal temperature') and be very unwell. The most important thing is to observe the overall condition of the child—the exact temperature is much less important.

The common signs and symptoms of serious illness in babies and young children are best summarised by what is known as 'A, B, C, Fluids in, and Fluids out'.

- 'A' stands for poor *arousal*, *alertness*, and *activity*;
- 'B' stands for *breathing difficulty*;
- 'C' stands for *circulation is poor*;
- 'Fluids in' refers to feeding less than half the normal amount over 24 hours; and
- 'Fluids out' refers to fewer than 4 wet nappies in 24 hours.

Although these signs and symptoms are relatively common in babies and small children, parents and carers should be aware that any baby or child with several of these features might have a serious illness.

The Box below provides more information about 'A, B, C, Fluids in, and Fluids out'.

'A, B, C, Fluids in, and Fluids out'

Alertness

When babies are awake they are normally alert. They respond to what is going on around them. They might be contented or they might be irritable, but they certainly respond.

Sick babies become drowsy and less responsive to normal stimulation. They might become 'floppy' with a weak whimpering cry. Sick infants move their arms and legs less than normal, and have less eye contact with their carers, or perhaps none at all.

Breathing

Healthy babies breathe easily and shallowly; excessive effort or noise indicates illness. The noise might be a grunt, a wheeze, a musical noise, or a harsh sound when the baby breathes in (which is called a 'stridor').

A baby with a serious illness can appear to be 'sucking in' the chest wall or sternum (breast bone). The baby can appear blue around the lips.

The number of breaths a baby takes each minute is not a factor that indicates serious illness.

Circulation

Poor circulation can make the baby's body look much paler than usual; or it might cause the baby to have cold legs up to the knees.

The normal response of a baby or young child with an infection is to be hot and flushed, but cold (or blue) hands and feet can occur in relatively minor infections. This does not mean the baby has a serious illness.

Fluids in

The total volume of fluid taken in over 24 hours needs to be estimated as a percentage of the baby's normal intake. Less than 50% of the baby's normal fluid intake should be considered as a sign of serious illness.

If a baby is breastfed, the frequency of feeding and the duration of active sucking needs to be considered. Mothers of breastfed babies are able to assess their baby's fluid intake as accurately as those who bottle-feed. The mother needs to consider how long the baby sucks for, and how strongly the baby sucks, and then compare this with the baby's normal feeding patterns

Fluids out

Fewer than four wet nappies in the past 24 hours indicates a higher risk of serious illness. More than five vomits in 24 hours (in a baby who does not normally vomit) also indicates serious illness.

Summary

If a parent or carer is worried about a baby or young child, it is always best to have the child seen by a doctor. If parents or carers think that a baby or young child might have a serious illness, they should go to the local doctor or to the nearest hospital emergency department immediately—whatever the time of day or night.

What is happening in a fever?

Beginnings of a fever

Most fevers are caused by infection from bacteria and viruses entering the body. They usually enter through the throat and respiratory tract in children (by breathing them in), but they can also gain access through cuts and scratches, or by eating infected food. Another common method of entry in small children is by rubbing the eyes.

> The hypothalamus is "re-set" to a higher temperature ... and "tells" the rest of the body to raise the temperature.

The white blood cells of the body attack the invading bacteria and viruses. When the invading organisms are destroyed, chemicals are produced. These chemicals (called 'pyrogens') stimulate a part of the brain called the hypothalamus which, among other things, controls the temperature of the body. The hypothalamus is 're-set' to a higher temperature by the circulating pyrogen chemicals, and the hypothalamus then 'tells' the rest of the body to raise the temperature and 'work hard' to overcome the infection.

Stages in a fever

The first stage in a developing fever is called the 'prodrome'. This occurs before a rash or other signs of infection are apparent. The child feels unwell, but does not have a temperature at this stage.

In the next stage of a developing fever, the child develops 'chills'. This occurs because the hypothalamus has been 're-set' by the pyrogens and is telling the rest of the body that the temperature should be higher (perhaps 39°C). The child therefore feels 'cold' because the temperature is not as high as it 'should' be (according to the re-set hypothalamus). In an attempt to get the temperature up, the child's muscles begin to work and the child develops typical 'chills and shivers'. During this stage, a child can have an elevated temperature (say 38°C) but still complain of 'feeling cold' (because the temperature is not as high as the hypothalamus is saying that it should be).

Stages in a fever

This part of the text discusses the stages in a fever. The stages in most fevers are:

- prodrome;
- chills;
- flushing; and
- sweating.

The next stage is 'flushing'. The temperature of the body has now risen to the 'revised' setting of the hypothalamus (39°C), and the child feels better again. But the child's skin is hot and dry, and the temperature is elevated.

The next stage is 'sweating'. This occurs because the body has temporarily overcome the first stage of the infection and the hypothalamus is 're-set' again—but at a somewhat lower temperature (say 38°C). The child's temperature is higher than this (39°C), so the child feels that he or she is 'too hot'. In response to this, the body tries to lower the temperature by sweating and evaporation.

During a developing infection, these variations can occur several times, and a child can feel that he or she is 'too cold' or 'too hot'. The child therefore has alternating phases of 'chills and shivers' and phases of being 'hot and sweaty'.

Effects of a fever in the body

A raised temperature assists the child's defences against infection. It increases the activity and distribution of white blood cells in attacking bacteria and viruses, and stimulates antibody production. A high temperature also limits the replication of some viruses. Some antibiotics also work better at a higher temperature. So lowering a temperature is not necessarily a good thing.

Lowering a temperature is not necessarily a good thing.

On the other hand, there are some harmful effects of a high temperature. It increases metabolic rate, heart rate, and respiratory rate. This can cause problems—especially in a child who already has heart or lung problems. A high temperature also increases fluid loss from sweating, and this can cause dehydration. Children are already more prone to dehydration than adults, and a fever can make this worse. A rapid rise in temperature can also be associated with a febrile convulsion (see 'Febrile convulsions', this chapter, page 15). Finally, a fever can cause discomfort and make a child feel unwell—although it might well be the underlying infection (sore throat, earache, and so on) that is the main cause of the discomfort.

Causes of fever

Common causes

The common causes of fever in children are listed in the Box below. Otitis media (middle ear infections) are clearly the most common cause of fever in children aged three years or less. Indeed, in small children who develop a fever, more than a third will have otitis media. About a quarter will have a 'non-specific illness'. The term 'non-specific illness' (see Box) refers to vague illnesses with no definite diagnosis—most of which are due to viral infections.

Common causes of fever in children

The most common causes of fever in children (aged 3 years or less) are:

- otitis media (37%)
- non-specific illness (25%)
- pneumonia (15%)
- recognisable viral illness (13%)
- recognisable bacterial illness (10%)

Uncommon causes

The majority of children who have a fever have a viral infection, and most are mild and non-threatening. However, it must be remembered that a small proportion of children with a fever (about 3%) will have a more serious bacterial infection (such as meningococcal disease). These require expert medical care. (See Chapter 3 'Rashes and Infectious Diseases', page 21, for more on meningococcal disease.)

Management of fever

Deciding whether to treat

It is not necessary to treat every fever. In deciding whether to treat a fever, a host of different circumstances has to be taken into account. It is not possible in a 'Basic Guide' book such as this to give a full account of every possible situation. However, some useful guidelines and tips can be given.

General wellbeing and past history

The most important thing to assess is the general wellbeing of the child. If a child appears well and happy, and if the child does not have any other significant medical problems (such as heart disease), there is usually no need to treat the fever in itself. However, if the child is miserable or if the child has other medical problems that might be made worse by the fever, it is appropriate to lower the fever. The Box on page 13 gives some examples.

Infants

A febrile young infant (that is, a child aged 1–3 months who has a fever) is at greater risk than older children.

All febrile infants under the age of one month should be admitted to hospital.

In general, all febrile infants under the age of one month should be admitted to hospital.

For those aged 1–3 months, expert medical assessment is required—including blood tests and other tests (such as lumbar puncture) to check for serious infection. After they have been assessed by experts, some febrile infants aged 1–3 months should be admitted to hospital, but some can be sent home. Infants who should be admitted include:

- those who appear to be unwell;
- those who are known to have other medical problems;
- those who have a past history of prematurity or treatment in a hospital neonatal unit; and
- those who have inadequate social support (such as unreliable parents, no transport back to hospital, no access to a phone, and so on).

Aims and methods of treatment

The main aims of treating a fever are to prevent dehydration and reduce discomfort (although discomfort might be due to the underlying cause of the infection, rather than the fever itself).

Treat or not treat?

In deciding whether to treat or not treat a fever, the most important thing to assess is the general wellbeing of the child. The following examples give a guide.

Case 1

An 18-month old boy has otitis media (ear infection) and a temperature of 39.8°C. He is sitting quietly watching a video and appears quite happy. He is drinking well and is well hydrated.

Would you treat this fever?

The answer is that this fever can be left alone. The little boy is quite well and happy. The fever, in itself, does not appear to be doing him any harm. However, he should be carefully monitored to ensure that he remains well.

Case 2

A 2-year-old girl has a urinary tract infection and a temperature of 39.1°C. The child is miserable and drinking poorly.

Would you treat this fever?

The answer is that this fever should be treated. Even though the temperature is lower than the temperature of the little boy in Case 1, this little girl is miserable and unhappy. And, because she is not drinking, she might well become dehydrated. This fever should be treated with paracetamol.

Case 3

A 3-year-old boy has a mild upper respiratory tract infection and a temperature of 38.7°C. The child is quite happy and is drinking well. However, the child is known to have a heart problem. This boy was born with a congenital cardiac abnormality and has a heart murmur.

Would you treat this fever?

The answer is that this fever should be treated. The little boy has heart problems, and it is not a good idea to let his heart work any harder. Lowering the boy's temperature with paracetamol will help to protect his heart from overwork.

It should be noted that lowering a temperature does not necessarily prevent a febrile convulsion; indeed it might increase the risk (see 'Prevention of febrile convulsions', page 17).

To achieve these aims, the most common method of treatment is to administer paracetamol (see below).

The child should also be given fluids and encouraged to rest—although there is no need to insist on rest if the child feels and looks reasonably well.

In general, light clothing is recommended because it is helpful in lowering a temperature. However, if the child is in the 'chills' stage and complains of feeling cold, he or she should be wrapped in a blanket until the 'chills' pass.

It is no longer recommended that children be sponged and actively cooled down with cold air.

Paracetamol

The most common treatment for a fever is paracetamol (known in the USA as 'acetaminophen'). The correct dose is 15 mg per kg (child's body weight) every 4 hours. No more than four doses should be given in 24 hours. The Box on page 14 explains how to calculate the correct dose.

Calculating dosage of paracetamol

The correct dosage is 15 mg per kg (child's body weight) every 4–6 hours (if required). No more than four doses should be given in 24 hours. To calculate the dose, we need to know the child's weight (in kg) and the strength of the paracetamol mixture being used (in mg/mL).

Child's weight

Let us suppose that the child weighs 20 kg.

Strength of paracetamol

Let us suppose that the paracetamol mixture is 120 mg/5 mL. This means that it contains 120 mg of paracetamol in every 5 mL of mixture. Or, in other words, it contains 24 mg of paracetamol in every 1 mL.

Dose of paracetamol required

The correct dose of paracetamol is 15 mg for every kilogram of body weight. The child weighs 20 kg, so this child requires 20 lots of 15 (mg) = 20 x 15 = 300 mg in total.

Calculating the volume of paracetamol to give

We wish to give 300 mg. The paracetamol mixture contains 24 mg in every 1 mL So we must divide the amount we wish to give (300 mg) by 24 to find out how many mL to give. This means we must divide 300 by 24 = 12.5 mL.

Answer

So this child requires 12.5 mL of the paracetamol mixture. This dose should be given every 4–6 hours (if required), but with no more than four doses in 24 hours.

Paracetamol can cause liver damage. Because of this risk, the maximum daily dosage should not be exceeded, and children should not be given paracetamol for more than two days without being assessed by a doctor.

Special care should be taken with obese children. Although these children have a 'heavy' body weight, most of this extra weight is in fat. Their livers are usually no bigger than those of children of normal weight. This means that a dose of paracetamol calculated on body weight alone might be too much for the liver of an obese child. These children should have a paracetamol dose to match their *age*, not their *weight*. A good general rule is as follows: if a child is obviously obese, give a paracetamol dose according to the child's *age*; but if a child is obviously underweight, give a paracetamol dose according to the child's *weight*. The Box on page 15 provides a useful 'rule' of thumb' for working out a child's 'expected' weight for age.

Paracetamol should only be used sparingly to relieve discomfort in mild short-term illnesses.

It should be noted that paracetamol does not always decrease a child's temperature. It should also be noted that a fever is a 'normal' part of the body's response to the infection and it is not necessarily helpful to reduce the temperature. For these reasons, it is recommended that paracetamol should only be used sparingly to relieve discomfort in mild short-term illnesses. There is a danger that children with more severe illnesses will be treated at home (with paracetamol) and not receive the medical management that they require.[1]

Weight for age

Rule of thumb

Although children differ in height and build, there is a handy 'rule of thumb' for estimating the 'expected' weight for a child of a certain age (up to about the age of 10 years). The 'rule of thumb' works like this:

Add 4 to the child's age, and then multiply by 2

Examples

Using the above 'rule of thumb' the 'expected' weight of a 6-year-old child can be calculated as follows:

age = 6

age plus 4 = 10

multiply by 2 = 20

The 'expected weight' of a 6-year-old child is therefore 20 kg.

For a 3 year-old child, the calculation goes as follows:

age = 3

age plus 4 = 7

multiply by 2 = 14

The 'expected weight' of a 3-year-old child is therefore 14 kg.

Please note that this 'rule of thumb' is a rough guide only, and normal children can differ from this 'expected' weight for age.

Ibuprofen

Ibuprofen is a non-steroidal anti-inflammatory agent (related to aspirin). The recommended dose is 10 mg per kg (child's body weight). This should be repeated every 6 hours (if required). It does have side-effects, and should not be used in children who have asthma. It is especially useful for treating conditions associated with acute inflammation—such as otitis media.

Febrile convulsions

Description of febrile convulsions

A febrile convulsion is a 'seizure' or 'fit' associated with a high temperature. It is a terrifying experience for a parent or carer to witness a febrile convulsion in a child. Many parents report that they feared that their child was dying. Many attempt CPR (cardiopulmonary resuscitation) to 'save' the child's life.

A febrile convulsion is a generalised spasm of the muscles of the body in a child with a high temperature (above 38°C). The child jerks around uncontrollably on a bed or floor, and appears to be unconscious or unresponsive.

It is very rare for a febrile convulsion to last more than ten minutes; in fact most febrile convulsions last less than three minutes.

Febrile convulsions

This part of the text discusses febrile convulsions under the following headings:

Incidence and frequency of febrile convulsions

Febrile convulsions are relatively common. About 3–5% of children (about 1 in 20) have a febrile convulsion at some stage in their lives.

Most occur between six months and six years of age. They usually start under 3–4 years of age. It is rare for a 4- or 5-year old to have a *first* febrile convulsion. However, if a child has a febrile convulsion at an earlier age, he or she might continue having them until about the age of six years.

Boys are twice as likely as girls to have a febrile convulsion.

Temperature changes and convulsions

The absolute height of a temperature cannot be used to predict a febrile convulsion. Some children will convulse with a temperature of 38°C whereas others will not convulse until the temperature reaches 40°C. And a child's personal 'pattern' can change—for example, a child might have previously had a convulsion with a temperature of 40°C, but then have a later convulsion with a temperature of only 38°C.

It's not how *high* a temperature gets, it's how *quickly* it gets there!

So the absolute height of a temperature cannot be used to predict a febrile convulsion. However, it does seem that a rapid rise in temperature *can* lead to a febrile convulsion. A child whose temperature rises slowly to 40°C might have no problems, but a child whose temperature rises rapidly from 36.5°C to 38.5°C might have a convulsion. In simple terms, it's not how *high* a temperature gets, it's how *quickly* it gets there!

Effects of febrile convulsions

Febrile convulsions are 'benign' conditions. This means that they do not have any long-lasting ill-effects and they do not cause death.

Most of the ill-effects from febrile convulsions occur in parents and carers! They can panic when a febrile convulsion occurs, and they can live in fear of another occurring at some time.

However, parents and carers can be reassured that febrile convulsions cause no long-term damage to children, and that children do *not* die from febrile convulsions.

Risk factors for febrile convulsions

Parents and carers are obviously concerned to know whether their children are likely to have a febrile convulsion. The risk factors differ for *first* convulsions and *repeat* convulsions. The Box below lists the risk factors that make a child 'more likely' to have a febrile convulsion.

Risk factors for febrile convulsions

First convulsion

A child is 'more likely' to have a first febrile convulsion if:

- there is a family history of febrile convulsions;
- the child spent more than a month in a neonatal unit after birth;
- the child has delayed development; or
- the child attends day care (because infections are more common in day-care centres).

Repeat convulsion

A child is 'more likely' to have another febrile convulsion if:

- the present illness continues (with 10–15% of children having two or more febrile convulsions in a single illness);
- the child is young (with 1-year-old children having a 50% chance of recurrence, and a 2-year-old child having a 30% chance of recurrence);
- the child's family has a history of febrile convulsions;
- the child's first convulsion occurred at a relatively low temperature; or
- the child's first convulsion occurred quickly (within one hour of developing a fever).

Causes of febrile convulsions

It used to be thought that the height of the temperature was a crucial factor in producing a febrile convulsion. However, as noted above, it is now apparent that a rapid rise in temperature is the most important factor. More than 30% of febrile convulsions occur when the parents are not even aware that the child has a fever.

Any infection can cause a febrile convulsion, but viral illnesses (especially herpes infections) commonly cause the sort of rapid rise in temperature that is associated with a febrile convulsion.

Prevention of febrile convulsions

Febrile convulsions cannot be prevented. Paracetamol and ibuprofen do *not* prevent febrile convulsions; in fact, the use of paracetamol and ibuprofen might even increase the risk of febrile convulsions in susceptible children.[2] Although the child's temperature is reduced by a dose of paracetamol (or ibuprofen), it then rises again when the medication wears off. In a susceptible child, a sudden rise in temperature (as the medication wears off) might trigger a convulsion.

Once a child has had a convulsion, there is no need to lower the temperature quickly. The child can be allowed to 'cruise along' with an elevated temperature (of say 38°C, or 39°C, or 40°C). Slight changes in temperature (even if already elevated) are unlikely to produce another convulsion. Remember that it is a sudden large *rise* in temperature that triggers a febrile convulsion.

It is a sudden large rise in temperature that triggers a febrile convulsion.

In the past, some children were given prophylactic ('preventive') medication to prevent recurrences of convulsions. This was usually a tranquilliser or sedative—such as diazepam ('Valium') or phenobarbitone ('phenobarb'). However, the side-effects of these medications—especially sedation and drowsiness—caused more problems than any benefits that might have been gained. For these reasons, prophylactic medication is no longer administered to prevent febrile convulsions.

Management of febrile convulsions

Ensure safety

The first step in managing a febrile convulsion is to ensure the safety of the child. If the child is on a bed, parents should ensure that the child cannot fall to the floor. If the child is on the floor, parents and carers should remove any objects (such as furniture) that might cause injury. The child should not be restrained. Nothing should be placed inside the child's mouth.

As soon as the jerking stops (usually after 2–3 minutes, but sometimes up to 10 minutes), the child should be placed on his or her side. Parents and carers should stay with the child until he or she wakes up.

Remain calm and reassure onlookers

Everyone should remain calm. Parents, carers, and others (such as members of the family or friends) should be reassured that the condition is not serious—even though it can be very frightening to observe. They can be told that the convulsion will soon cease, and they should be reassured that it is not life-threatening and will not cause any long-term medical problems.

Observe carefully

The convulsion should be carefully observed. The nature and the duration of the convulsion should be noted—so this information can be passed onto medical staff.

If the convulsion occurs in a clinic or hospital where medical equipment is available, there is no need to administer any 'emergency' medical treatment—such as oxygen or suction. This does no good, and it only causes parents to become more alarmed. Indeed, it gives the 'wrong message' to parents. If parents observe nurses and other carers using oxygen and suction, the parents will think that they need to administer emergency medical treatment themselves if a convulsion occurs again.

When convulsion has stopped

When the convulsion has ceased, the child should be placed on his or her side. The airway (mouth and upper throat) should be checked, and cleared if necessary.

The child will be drowsy for a while—perhaps for 10–30 minutes. During this time the child should be placed on his or her side, and observed.

If the convulsion does not stop within ten minutes (as 95% do), parents and carers should call an ambulance. If in hospital or a clinic, it might be necessary for a doctor or nurse to administer an anticonvulsant medication.

Medical attention

Any child who has a febrile convulsion needs to be seen by a doctor. Although febrile convulsions do not, in themselves, cause any serious problems, some children will have a serious underlying problem that has not been previously detected. Doctors and nurses will decide if any special investigations are required. In addition, the parents or carer will require reassurance and education on the condition.

In general, if a child has a febrile convulsion, parents and carers should be advised to call an ambulance and seek medical attention. This is good advice whether the child is at home, school, or in a day-care centre.

Any child who has a febrile convulsion needs to be seen by a doctor.

Final messages

Treat the child, not the thermometer!

The most important final message of this chapter is that parents and carers who have a child with a fever should focus on the child's general health and behaviour—rather than the measurement on a thermometer. It doesn't really matter what the child's temperature is. What does matter is the child's general demeanour.

The answers to the following sorts of questions are more important than the child's temperature:

- Is the child alert and active (a good sign) or is the child passive and lethargic (a bad sign)?
- Is the child flushed and irritable (which are to be expected in a child with a fever) or is the child pale and lethargic (which is a bad sign in a child with a fever)?

It should be remembered that the height of a child's temperature bears no relation to how sick the child is. Some children can be very ill with meningitis and have a temperature of only 37.5°C, whereas other children can have a mild viral illness and have a temperature of 40°C.

The height of a child's temperature bears no relation to how sick the child is.

In summary, treat the child, not the thermometer!

Avoid unnecessary medications

Although paracetamol and ibuprofen are useful in relieving some distressing symptoms, they should not be overused. Fresh dilute orange juice and a cuddle are much safer alternatives than unnecessary medications.[3]

Notes

1. This advice comes from the (Australian) Consultative Council on Obstetrics and Paediatric Mortality (1998).

2. For more on how paracetamol and ibuprofen might increase the risk of a febrile convulsion, see: (i) van Stuijvenberg, M., Derksen-Labsen, G., Steyerberg, E.W. et al. 1998, 'Randomised controlled trial of ibuprofen syrup administered during febrile illness to prevent febrile seizure occurrence; *Pediatrics*, 102:5, p. 51; (ii) van Esch, A. Steyerberg, E.W. Moll, H.A. et al. 2000, 'A study of the efficacy of antipyretic drugs in the prevention of febrile seizure occurrence', *Ambulatory Child Health*, 6:1, 19–25; and (iii) El-Radhi, A. & Barry, W. 2003, 'Do antipyretics prevent febrile convulsions?' *Archives of Disease in Childhood*, 88:638–42.

3. This comment comes from Hewson, P. 2000, 'Paracetamol: Evidence mounts against its indiscriminate or persistent use in childhood', *Australian Prescriber*, 23:3, 60–1.

Chapter 3

Rashes and Infectious Diseases

Introduction

Rashes are common. Children get rashes virtually from the day they are born. Many are of no account. For example, many infants have little so-called 'milk spots' on the face soon after birth; these are of no importance and soon fade. But children get many other rashes during childhood, and parents and carers can often be concerned.

This chapter describes common rashes of childhood and offers practical advice on assessing the rash, diagnosing the cause (if possible), and knowing what to do.

History of the rash

In making a diagnosis of a rash, doctors and nurses first take a *history*. Doctors and nurses use the word 'history' to mean the 'story' of what has happened. This is basically a description of the sequence of events that led up to the rash. This 'history' can also include 'past history' (whether the child has ever had any other medical problems) and 'family history' (whether other members of the family have any rashes or other relevant medical problems).

In assessing a rash in a child, parents and carers obviously do not have to take a full medical history in the same way as a health professional would do. However, parents and carers can obtain a lot of information—which could be useful for themselves or for health professionals—by observing the child carefully and thinking back over the sequence of events involved in the 'history'. The sorts of questions that parents or carers should ask themselves are listed in the Box on page 22. More information on these questions is provided in the text that follows.

Parents and carers can obtain a lot of information—which could be useful for themselves or for health professionals.

Framework of chapter

This chapter discusses rashes and infectious diseases. The chapter discusses the following subjects:

Questions to be asked

Parents and carers should ask themselves the following questions about a child with a rash:

- What happened first?
- What does the rash look like, and how did it start?
- Is the rash itchy?
- Has the child been given any medications recently?
- Does the child have any other medical illnesses?
- Has the child had any contact with other people who are sick?

The sorts of questions to be answered include:

- *What happened first?* Parents and carers should ask themselves whether the child had other signs and symptoms before the rash appeared—such as being irritable and miserable, or having a fever.
- *What does the rash look like, and how did it start?* Different rashes have different features and distribution on the body. Parents and carers should consider whether the rash began as little spots and later became 'blotchy', or was it the same all along? Has it developed into blisters and crusts? Did it begin on the face and work down the body (as measles does), or did it begin on the chest and extend out to the limbs (as chickenpox typically does)? In answering these questions, it is important to observe the child carefully—in good, natural light (not under fluorescent light) if possible.
- *Is the rash itchy?* Some rashes are itchy and some are not.

- *Has the child been given any medications recently?* This might be important because some medications can cause an allergic rash. Other medications might alter signs and symptoms.
- *Does the child have any other medical illnesses?* Underlying medical problems can affect the onset of a rash and its subsequent history.
- *Has the child had any contact with other people who are sick?* Relatives, friends, or contacts at school or day care might have an infectious illness. Or the child might have recently travelled overseas to an area in which infectious disease is more common.

Early signs and symptoms of concern

Because rashes are common, it is often difficult for parents and carers to decide whether a particular rash is something to be concerned about. In most cases this can only be decided by getting a proper diagnosis from a health professional. However, there are some signs and symptoms that should make parents and carers more concerned. These features do not mean that the situation is necessarily life-threatening. However, parents and carers should be more concerned if they notice the features listed in the Box below.

Signs and symptoms of concern

There are some signs and symptoms associated with a rash that should make parents and carers more concerned. These features do not necessarily mean that the situation is life-threatening. However, parents and carers should be more concerned if they notice the following.

- Fever: In general, if a child has a rash and a fever, the illness is likely to be more significant.
- Young age: Any illness is potentially more serious in an infant or very young child. This includes illnesses with rashes.
- 'Toxic-looking': In general, if children 'look sick', they are sick.
- Enlarged glands: If a child has swollen glands, the illness is more likely to be significant. These glands can be felt most easily around the throat and neck, under the arms, and in the groins.
- Erythema: The word 'erythema' refers to redness of the skin. If a child has generalised erythema of the skin (underlying the rash), the illness is likely to be more significant.
- Petechiae and purpura: Petechiae (pronounced 'p-TEEK-ee-eye') are small, flat, red-brown spots on the skin. They are important in diagnosing meningococcal disease. (For more information on recognising petechiae, see the Box on page 24.)
- Mouth ulcers: Children with painful mouth ulcers sometimes can't eat and drink—thus increasing the risk of dehydration. Even relatively trivial illnesses can cause significant problems in small children if the illness causes mouth ulcers and the child refuses to drink (or cannot drink).
- Severe localised pain: Any child with severe localised pain (with or without a rash) requires medical attention.
- Arthralgia: The term 'arthralgia' refers to 'sore joints'. Some joint pain is common in infectious illnesses, but severe arthralgia requires medical assessment.
- Recent new medications: Allergic reactions to medications can be serious. If a child develops a rash soon after taking a new medication, the medication should be stopped and a medical opinion should be obtained.
- Other medical problems: If a child has any other significant medical problems or medical treatment, especially anything that reduces immunity (for example, chemotherapy for cancer), an infectious disease is more likely to cause problems.

Describing a rash

There are various technical terms that are used to describe rashes. There is no need for parents and carers to know these technical words in detail. It is quite sufficient for a parent or carer to be able to describe a rash in relatively simple terms—for example: 'This child has small, slightly raised, red spots on the chest and abdomen'. If parents or carers can accurately describe a rash in this way, this indicates that they have observed carefully and closely. And this sort of information is quite sufficient to help a doctor or nurses make a diagnosis.

However, even though the technical terms are not strictly necessary, parents and carers might like to know what these terms mean. Sometimes a parent or carer receives a letter from a doctor in which these words are used. Or perhaps a parent or carer has been reading a medical book and comes across these words. For these reasons, the meanings of these technical terms are explained in the Box below.

Some technical terms to describe a rash

The 'ordinary' meanings of the technical terms that are used to describe a rash are given below.

Erythema (or erythematous)

The term 'erythema' simply means 'red'.

Macule

A 'macule' is a small, flat area (or 'spot') of discoloured skin (usually less than 5 mm in diameter).

Maculo–papular

The term 'maculo–papular' refers to a combination of small flat 'spots' and raised 'spots' on the skin. This sort of rash is typical of measles.

Nodule

A 'nodule' is a larger swelling on the skin surface (usually more than 5 mm in diameter). It extends deep into skin, and is usually firm to the touch.

Papule

A 'papule' is a small, raised area of skin (less than 5 mm). It usually has a domed top (although it can be flat).

Petechiae

Petechiae (pronounced 'p-TEEK-ee-eye') are small, red-brown, flat macules (see above) up to 2 mm in diameter. It is important to note that they do not blanch (turn white) when pressure is applied with a finger—in contrast to most rashes in children which DO fade when pressure is applied. Petechiae are caused by tiny spots of blood gathered under the surface of the skin. They are important in diagnosing meningococcal disease.

Purpura

'Purpura' means areas of little petechiae joined together. These are therefore larger areas (usually more than 2 mm) of bleeding under the skin.

Pustule

A 'pustule' is a vesicle (see below) containing yellow fluid. This fluid usually consists of serum (blood fluid), white blood cells, and the virus that has caused the original infection. The presence of a pustule

(continued)

(continued)

does NOT mean that the rash has 'become infected' with bacteria; pustules are an 'expected' event in many viral illnesses.

Vesicle

A 'vesicle' is a papule (see above) with a fluid-filled centre. Vesicles are typical of chickenpox rash and 'cold sores'.

Chickenpox

Highly contagious

Chickenpox (or 'varicella') is a highly contagious disease caused by the *Herpes zoster* virus (also called the 'varicella–zoster virus'). Because it is so highly contagious, it spreads rapidly among susceptible people who have not had chickenpox (or immunisation) in the past. For example, if there is a case of chickenpox in a family, there is a 90% chance that other susceptible members of the family will get the disease.

Chickenpox is usually a mild disease of short duration in otherwise healthy children. However, it can be a more severe disease in susceptible adults and in children whose immune systems are affected by medications or illness. For the protection of such people, parents should advise school or childcare authorities if their child has chickenpox.

For the protection of other people, parents should advise school or childcare authorities if their child has chickenpox.

The disease is so contagious that, by the age of 12 years, about 75% of non-immunised children have had chickenpox, and 95% of people will have had the disease by adulthood (although these percentages will change with the relatively recent introduction of vaccines).

Incubation period and early illness

The time from when the child first contracts an infectious disease until the rash appears is called the 'incubation period'. The average incubation period for chickenpox is about 14 days, although it can be as little as 7 days or as long as 21 days. The child is thought to be infectious from about three days before the rash appears. They can pass chickenpox onto other people at this time.

About three days before the rash appears, most children develop a fever and feel unwell. The fever can be quite high (39°C). The child might also develop other signs and symptoms before the rash appears—such as headache, sore throat, and cough. However, in some cases, the child can remain well until the rash appears; in these cases, the first sign of the illness is the appearance of the rash.

Rash

The rash usually first appears on the trunk (chest and abdomen), and then spreads to the face and extremities. It often affects the mucous membranes of the body—such as the inside lining of the mouth. This can cause difficulties with eating and drinking. New spots usually stop appearing about 4–5 days after the first spots appeared.

It is an itchy rash that begins as macules ('flat spots'), which later become papules ('raised spots') and then form vesicles ('clear blisters'). These vesicles then turn into pustules ('cloudy blisters'). The rash occurs in 'crops', and it is possible to see a mixture of these different sorts of rash 'spots' (macules, papules, vesicles, and pustules) in each 'crop'. The last stage (pustules) eventually form crusts, which fall off after about 7–10 days.

The rash occurs in "crops", and it is possible to see a mixture of different sorts of rash "spots" in each "crop".

Technical terms used in this chapter

This chapter uses some technical terms as a 'shorthand' way of describing what happens in certain infectious diseases. Most of these are explained in the text, but this list might also be helpful.

Antibiotics
Medications that kill bacteria

Benign
Not dangerous

Incubation period
The time from when a child gets an infection until the child becomes unwell

Prodrome
The early signs and symptoms of illness before a rash appears. Typical prodrome signs and symptoms are fever, runny, nose, and cough

Recurrent
Can come back again

Self-limiting
Something that goes away on its own

Sign
Something that a parent or carer notices in a sick child (such as a rash)

Susceptible
People who might get an infectious disease because they have not had it before, or because they have not had an immunisation, or because they have some other medical problem

Symptomatic treatment
Treatment that aims to relieve symptoms (such as itch or pain) without attempting to cure the cause

Symptom
Something that the sick child complains about but other people cannot see (such as pain)

Spread of disease

Chickenpox is mainly spread by coughing and sneezing. But it can also be spread by virus in the fluid in the pustules and crusts of the rash—by direct touching or by 'airborne' transmission (such as from shaking contaminated clothing or bedding).
A child with chickenpox is therefore infectious until every last part of the rash has dried out and formed a crust. It is also possible for chickenpox to be spread across the placenta from an infected pregnant woman to her fetus.

A child with chickenpox is infectious until every last part of the rash has dried out and formed a crust.

Care of child with chickenpox

Most children with chickenpox are cared for at home. When the diagnosis is made, they should be isolated from susceptible people—especially those who might be at greater risk. These include elderly people, pregnant women, and those whose immune systems are affected by medications or illness. Authorities at school or day care should be notified.

The Box below summarises the care of children with chickenpox. The following text gives further information.

Care of a child with chickenpox

This part of the text describes the care of a child with chickenpox. The text gives more information on the following:

- isolate the child from susceptible people;
- manage the itch;
- watch fluid intake; and
- never give aspirin.

The itch can be treated with antihistamine medications and with baths containing 'anti-itch' solutions. Pharmacists can advise on these medications. The child's fingernails should be kept short and clean to avoid secondary infection from scratching the itchy rash. Appropriate diversional activities—such as playing quiet games or watching television—can also help to prevent unnecessary itching. The child should also be kept cool; overheating should be avoided.

Fluid intake should be carefully monitored to ensure that the child is drinking enough. This is especially important if the child has rash in the mouth. Soothing fluids, such as jelly and icy poles, are a good idea.

Fluid intake should be carefully monitored to ensure that the child is drinking enough—especially if the child has rash in the mouth.

Children with chickenpox can be miserable and 'grizzly'. However, they should *never* be treated with aspirin (or related medications called 'salicylates'). If children who have chickenpox are given aspirin they can develop a condition called 'Reye's syndrome'. Although this is rare, it is a serious disease; in fact, about a third of people with Reye's syndrome can die. It is more likely to occur in children and teenagers with chickenpox, influenza, and other viral illnesses who are treated with aspirin (and other salicylates). Because it is often difficult to make a precise diagnosis in the early stages of these illnesses, especially before a typical rash has appeared, *no child or teenager should ever be given aspirin for a fever*. If treatment is required, paracetamol or ibuprofen are the medications of choice in these cases.

No child or teenager should ever be given aspirin for a fever.

Complications

Chickenpox is usually a mild and self-limiting disease; however, in some cases, complications can occur. Parents and carers should therefore be watchful for signs and symptoms of complications of chickenpox. These include:

- rash lesions in the eyes;
- secondary bacterial infections of itchy rash lesions;
- pneumonia (chest infection); and
- neurological (brain) complications.

If the child develops *rash lesions in the eyes* (which is unusual), referral to an eye specialist is required.

Secondary bacterial infection of the chickenpox rash can be serious because it can cause infection of the blood. This is usually caused by excessive scratching of the rash with dirty fingernails. The rash becomes very red and inflamed, and the infected 'spots' become much bigger and 'angrier'. Referral to a doctor is required for possible antibiotic treatment.

Secondary bacterial infection of the chickenpox rash is usually caused by excessive scratching of the rash with dirty fingernails.

Serious *pneumonia* from chickenpox is uncommon, although a mild chest infection can occur in many cases. A cough is common in chickenpox, but if a child with chickenpox develops a severe cough and breathlessness, medical attention should be obtained.

The *neurological complications* of chickenpox can vary from mild problems that are self-limiting (that is, they go away after a few days or a week) to more serious problems. Signs and symptoms can include headache, photophobia (dislike of bright light), and unsteadiness when walking. In severe cases, a child can occasionally become very ill. Deaths can occur, but this is very rare. If a child with chickenpox develops any of the signs and symptoms of neurological complications—such as severe headache, photophobia, and unsteadiness when walking—medical attention should be obtained.

Chickenpox in pregnancy

Because chickenpox is a common disease in childhood, some mothers and child-carers who look after these children will be pregnant with another child. These women will be understandably concerned about the effect of chickenpox on their pregnancy.

They can be reassured that exposure to chickenpox during pregnancy is usually 'benign' (not serious)—especially if the woman is immune to the disease as a result of previous infection or immunisation. There are two times of risk.

The first is in the first 20 weeks of pregnancy. This can (rarely) cause damage to the developing fetus. However, the risk is much less than with other infectious diseases (such as rubella). A pregnant woman who is immune to chickenpox (from previous exposure or immunisation) is unlikely to have any problems.

The second 'risk period' is around the time of birth. If a pregnant woman develops chickenpox from about seven days before delivery until about 28 days after delivery, the newborn child can also develop the disease. In a minority of cases, this can be serious for the newborn infant. Women who are getting close to delivery, or those who have just given birth, should therefore avoid contact with chickenpox. However, a pregnant woman who is immune to chickenpox (from previous exposure or immunisation) is unlikely to have any problems—because she will provide antibodies to her newborn. If the woman is breastfeeding, this should be continued.

Women who are getting close to delivery, or those who have just given birth, should therefore avoid contact with chickenpox.

Immunisations

Immunisations for chickenpox have now been developed. These should be administered to the child between 12 and 18 months of age. 'Catch-up' immunisations can be given to older children who have not had the illness. If the chickenpox immunisation is not given on the same day as other immunisations it must not be given sooner than four weeks later.

Immunisation is usually recommended for people who are especially at risk—such as those whose immune systems are affected by illness or medications, or adults who are involved in professional child care, including teachers and healthcare workers.

Shingles

Cause

Shingles is caused by a 'reactivation' of the *Herpes zoster* virus in a person who has previously had chickenpox. The virus remains dormant in the body for many years, and 'flares up' later in life.

The vast majority of cases occur in adults. Only 1% of cases occur in children under 12 years of age, and 81% occur in adults older than 40 years.

Signs and symptoms

Shingles begins as a 'tingling' feeling, or itch, or pain—usually on the chest or abdomen (although it can occur elsewhere, such as on the face). It then develops into a rash with red spots, blisters, and (later) crusts. It can be very painful and debilitating, especially in older people.

Spread

The *Herpes zoster* virus is in the blisters of shingles, and can thus be spread to other people. Susceptible children and adults—that is, those who have not had chickenpox before—can therefore develop chickenpox from contact with a person who has active shingles. However, people who have chickenpox cannot cause shingles in other people—because shingles develops much later, after the virus has been 'dormant' in the body for a long time.

Cold sores

Common cold sores

So-called 'cold sores' are caused by infection with the *Herpes simplex* virus. They are contagious, blistering, painful 'spots' that commonly occur on the mouth and lips—although they can occur in other parts of the body (such as elsewhere on the face and on the sexual organs). They can also occur in the eyes (on the cornea) and, occasionally, in the brain. The most common site of infection in children is in and around the mouth.

Spread of cold sores

The virus is spread by close personal contact with an infected person—such as kissing. Once a child has been infected with the cold-sore virus, the sores can be recurrent (that is, they can come back again). This is often associated with the child being stressed or unwell with other illnesses.

The virus is spread by close personal contact with an infected person. Once a child has been infected with the cold-sore virus, the sores can be recurrent.

Rarely, the *Herpes simplex* virus can spread to other parts of the body. If it spreads to the brain this can cause a very serious illness known as 'herpes encephalitis'. Newborn infants and children whose immune systems are affected by medication or illness are most at risk. It is therefore advisable that people with cold sores (adults and children) should avoid contact with newborn infants.

Treatment

The treatment of cold sores is largely symptomatic—that is, relief of pain and discomfort. Analgesics ('pain-killers') and anaesthetic mouthwashes and gels can help. In severe cases, anti-viral medications can be prescribed by a doctor.

Hand, foot, and mouth disease

A mild contagious illness

Hand, foot, and mouth disease is a common, mild illness of children caused by a Coxsackie virus. Its proper name is 'vesicular exanthem'.

Signs and symptoms

The illness is so mild that many children are not even diagnosed as having a disease. Other children develop a mild fever, sore throat, and loss of appetite.

The illness is so mild that many children are not even diagnosed as having a disease.

As the name suggests, the most prominent feature is the presence of blisters on the palms of the hands, the soles of the feet, and in the mouth. The blisters are small and reddened, with a whitish centre. They are not usually painful or itchy, and usually disappear spontaneously after a few days to a week.

Spread

The virus is spread by direct contact or by droplet. The child is infectious while the blisters remain filled with fluid. However, the child's faeces can remain infectious for several weeks. Parents and carers can catch the illness from children.

Treatment

Treatment is symptomatic—that is, aimed to alleviate any unpleasant symptoms (such as sore throat). The blisters on the hands and feet can be covered with dressings and gloves/mittens—and then allowed to dry up naturally.

Not foot and mouth!

Of course, this disease is *not* the same as the well-known contagious animal disease 'foot and mouth'!

Erythema multiforme

Distinctive rash

The term 'erythema multiforme' means, literally, 'redness in many shapes'. The illness has a distinctive sort of rash, and this enables the diagnosis to be made.

The rash can occur, quite suddenly, anywhere on the body—including the face, chest, abdomen, and limbs. The most common sites are the palms and soles of the feet, the 'backs' of the hands, the limbs, and the face.

The rash 'spots' are described as typical 'target lesions'. This means that they have a 'ringed' appearance similar to the well-known 'bull's-eye target'—although the edges of the 'spots' are not necessarily circular. They can be of various sizes and shapes. Sometimes they come together to form large 'blotches' on the skin.

In mild erythema multiforme, there are usually no other signs and symptoms. There is usually no fever, and the rash is not usually itchy or painful.

Typical "target lesions" have a "ringed" appearance similar to the well-known "bull's-eye target"—although the edges are not necessarily circular.

Mild and severe erythema multiforme

Most cases of erythema multiforme are mild. The rash usually goes away in 7–10 days. Less commonly, the condition can be very severe. This involves the rash spreading into the mouth and eyes. Severe erythema multiforme can be life-threatening—but this is relatively rare.

Causes

Erythema multiforme can occur in children and adults—although it is rare at less than three years of age and more than 50 years of age. It is caused by an 'allergic-type' skin reaction to something in the child's environment. The most common causes are:

- infections; and
- medications.

Infections that can cause erythema multiforme include *Herpes simplex* ('cold sore virus') and *Mycoplasma pneumoniae* (a form of pneumonia). Other infections can also be involved.

Medications that can cause the illness include penicillin, sulphonamides ('sulphur drugs'), barbiturates, and phenytoin. Other medications can also be involved.

In about half the cases, the original cause is never found.

Treatment

The most important aspect of treatment is to remove the cause (if possible). For example, if a child develops erythema multiforme after starting on a course of antibiotics, the medication should be stopped and a medical opinion should be obtained.

In most cases, no other treatment is required. The problem usually clears up on its own.

Impetigo

'School sores'

Impetigo is more commonly known as 'school sores'. As the name indicates, these sores are most common among school-age children (usually aged about 4–7 years).

A typical "school sore" has a reddish edge and a characteristic yellowish "crusty scab" on top.

They can occur anywhere on the body, but are most commonly found on the face (especially around the mouth and chin) and hands.

The sores usually begin as small blisters. These 'burst' and leak a cloudy, yellowish fluid that dries on the skin—forming a 'crust' or 'scab'. A typical 'school sore' thus has a reddish edge and a characteristic yellowish 'crusty scab' on top.

Cause

Impetigo is caused by infection with bacteria—either staphylococcus or streptococcus. The bacteria are spread from sore to sore, or from child to child, by the child scratching or 'picking' at the sore and passing it on. The child is infectious while there are sores present on the skin.

Treatment

Impetigo usually requires treatment with antibiotics—so a visit to the doctor is usually required. Antibiotic ointment can be used for a few isolated sores, but a special form of oral penicillin called 'flucloxacillin' is usually required if there are more than one or two sores present.

It is very important that children do not touch the sores at all.

Apart from antibiotics, the most important aspect of treatment is to stop children spreading the infection (on their own bodies, or to others) by scratching and 'picking' at the sores. It is very important that children do not touch the sores at all.

Any people (such as parents or carers) who do touch the sores or surrounding skin should immediately wash their hands thoroughly.

The child can be allowed to return to school when antibiotic treatment has been started. However, the sores should be covered with gauze dressings or clothes. Plastic dressings (such as

'Band-aids') are not recommended because they cause sweating and this encourages the bacteria to grow.

Measles

No longer common

Measles is also known as 'rubeola' or 'morbilli'. It is an extremely contagious viral illness spread by respiratory droplets. It used to be a very common disease, and virtually all children used to get measles at some stage. However, with the advent of immunisation against the disease, very few cases of 'true' measles are seen today (although people often inaccurately claim that their child has 'measles'). In fact, the most common age group for measles today is 18–30 years. This is because most people under 18 are immunised, and most people over 30 have had the disease.

Typical presentation

A typical case of measles can be diagnosed from the history, the appearance of the face, and the rash. In fact, when measles was common, doctors and nurses were taught how to diagnose the condition simply by looking for a typical 'measles face'—a red-eyed and miserable child with a runny nose and a red rash.

The 'incubation period' (from time of infection to becoming unwell) is about 10–14 days. This is followed by a 'prodrome' (illness before the rash appears) of about 2–4 days. The child then develops fever, cough, runny nose, and conjunctivitis ('red eyes'). This combination of signs and symptoms makes the child appear typically 'red-eyed and miserable'.

A typical "measles face"—a red-eyed and miserable child with a runny nose and a red rash.

The rash usually starts on the face and then 'moves downwards' to the upper chest. It eventually becomes generalised. As it spreads downwards, it gradually clears up where it was previously. The rash thus clears from the face first.

The rash is technically described as an 'erythematous maculo-papular rash'; this means that it consists of a mixture of flat and raised red spots. (See the Box on page 24 for an explanation of these and other technical terms.)

Complications of measles

As noted above, measles used to be so common that virtually all children had the disease at some stage. However, it did have complications—some of which were very serious. Even though the rate of serious complications was relatively 'low' (perhaps only 1 in every 100 cases), there were so many children getting measles that even a relatively 'low' rate of complications involved a large number of children in the total population. For example, about 1% of children with measles developed encephalitis (measles brain infection). About 10–15% of these children died, and about 15–40% of survivors were left with severe brain damage. So even though the rate of complications was 'low' (only 1% overall), there were thousands of children involved every year. It was therefore decided that immunisation should be provided against this previously common illness.

Apart from encephalitis (brain infection), other complications of measles include otitis media (ear infection) and pneumonia.

It is therefore strongly recommended that all children be immunised against this potentially serious disease.

Treatment

With immunisation having been so successful, it is unlikely that many parents or carers will have to care for a child with measles. However, in general, treatment is symptomatic (managing unpleasant symptoms), together with fluids and rest until the illness clears up. This usually takes 2–3 weeks.

Molluscum contagiosum

Benign and self-limiting

Molluscum contagiosum is a viral infection of the skin that occurs most commonly in school-age children. It is benign (not dangerous in itself) and self-limiting (will eventually go away of its own accord). However, the 'spots' can cause cosmetic concern to both children and parents/carers. Some schools and child-care centres will not allow children to remain while they have visible 'spots'.

Typical appearance

The viral infection of the skin is spread by direct contact, but is slow-growing (usually weeks to months). It produces small 'pearl-like' raised 'spots'. These have a flat top and a central creamy-coloured 'core'. These can occur anywhere, but the face, trunk, and hands are common sites. The 'spots' can be single, or they can occur in small crops.

Treatment

No treatment is necessary. The child's body will mount an immune response, and the 'spots' of molluscum contagiosum always go away of their own accord over a period of months to years.

In a few cases, children and parents might wish to have them treated because there are so many, or because the child is being teased for having 'warts'. There are various treatments available (such as freezing or simple surgery), but these treatments can cause discomfort, and treatment is not usually recommended unless the child or parents are very keen to have something done.

Treatment is not usually recommended unless the child or parents are very keen to have something done.

Roseola infantum

Common disease of infants

Roseola infantum is a common viral illness of young children caused by infection with a Herpes virus. The disease is spread by respiratory droplets.

The most common age for onset is about 7–13 months, although older children (up to about three years) can develop the condition. Most children have had the condition by the age of two years. In some cases, parents and carers do not realise that the child has had the illness.

Fever and rash

A relatively high fever (up to 40°C) is common with this illness. The child typically has a fever for 2–4 days before the rash appears. However, the child is not usually miserable or unwell. The fever goes away as the rash appears.

The rash consists of small pink spots ('maculo-papular') on the chest and abdomen. It does not usually extend to the face or limbs. The rash fades away after a few hours or a few days.

Treatment

No treatment is necessary. The illness goes away of its own accord without any ill-effects.

A small proportion of children with this illness do have a febrile convulsion during the initial fever stage. Despite this, the fever does not have to be treated if the child does not appear to be unwell (see 'Chapter 2, 'Fevers and Febrile Convulsions', page 7).

Slapped cheek disease

Typical appearance

The proper name for this disease, which is caused by infection with a Parvovirus, is 'erythema infectosum'. The term 'slapped cheek disease' describes the typical appearance of the rash. The child develops red, rosy facial cheeks—as though he or she has been slapped on the face.

There is usually no preceding 'prodrome'—that is, the child does not usually develop a fever or unpleasant symptoms. The appearance of the rash is usually the first sign of the illness. It later spreads to the trunk and extremities.

The disease is self-limiting and is not serious in children, but it can be significant if contracted by a pregnant woman (see below, page 36) for more on this.

The child develops red, rosy facial cheeks—as though slapped on the face.

Transmission and stages in illness

The virus is spread by respiratory droplets and direct contact. There is an incubation period of about 4–14 days.

The illness typically has three stages, but not all stages occur in every case.

- Stage 1: The rash appears on the face—producing a 'slapped cheek' appearance. This lasts 1–4 days.
- Stage 2: The rash spreads to the trunk and extremities. The rash consists of small pink-red 'spots' that are flat or slightly raised ('maculo-papular'). It is sometimes described as having a 'lace-like' appearance. This lasts for about seven days.
- Stage 3: The rash fades, but it can come back if the skin is exposed to irritants (heat, cold, friction). This stage can last for weeks or months, but gradually goes away.

Treatment

The illness does not usually cause any significant problems in children. Treatment is symptomatic.

Pregnant women

Exposure to a child with 'slapped cheek disease' can be a problem for pregnant women who are not immune to the disease as a result of previous exposure. There is no immunisation, but it is estimated that 60–70% of pregnant women are already immune to the disease.

If a pregnant woman is exposed to the disease at home or at child-care, she should have blood tests and be carefully monitored.

The virus causes damage to immature red blood cells, and this can cause anaemia in the pregnant woman *and* in her fetus. This is usually not serious, but in more severe cases, there can be significant complications. In the first trimester of pregnancy, infection can cause miscarriage. Later in the pregnancy, infection can cause severe anaemia in the fetus.

If a pregnant woman is exposed to the disease at home or at child-care, she should have blood tests and be carefully monitored.

Urticaria ('hives')

Common condition

Urticaria (or 'hives') is a common allergic reaction of the skin. It is estimated that about 10–20% of all people have an episode of urticaria at some stage in their lives.

The substance that causes the reaction (called the 'allergen') can be almost anything. It can be food, medications, soaps, plants, animals, infections, and so on. In many cases the allergen is never clearly identified. In other cases, children are known to be especially allergic to a particular sort of allergen.

Appearance

The rash consists of pale or red swelling of the skin. It is usually extremely itchy. It can occur anywhere on the body. If it occurs around the eyes, lips, or throat the swelling can be severe. In some cases it can be dangerous. The skin reaction can last for hours, days, or weeks.

Treatment

Mild cases require no treatment. In moderate cases, treatment with antihistamines might be needed to stop the reaction and decrease itching. In severe cases—such as swelling around the throat—emergency medical care can be required.

For more on emergency treatment of allergic reactions, see Chapter 13, 'Emergency Care', page 123.

Meningococcal disease

Frightening, but rare

There has been a great deal of publicity about meningococcal disease, and it *is* a frightening disease. However, it should be remembered that it is a relatively rare disease. Only about 3 people in every 100,000 in the population will contract the disease in their lifetimes. Of these, most recover completely. Only about 10% die of the disease, and a further 20% are left with a significant disability. So it is a relatively rare disease and only a very small proportion of the population are significantly affected by it.

However, meningococcal disease *is* a frightening disease. There are several reasons for this:

- it strikes young children (under five years) and adolescents/young adults (15–29 years) more often than other age groups;
- it is difficult to diagnose (often appearing to be only a mild viral illness, or gastroenteritis, or even merely 'aches and pains' in the early stages); and
- it can cause serious injury and death quite quickly.

It is therefore very important that parents and carers are aware of the signs and symptoms of meningococcal disease.

Types and cause

The term 'meningococcal disease' includes two types of illness:

- meningitis and encephalitis (inflammation of the spinal cord and brain); and
- septicaemia (blood poisoning).

The two can occur separately, or together. Septicaemia (with or without meningitis) is more likely to cause death.

Meningococcal disease is most common among young children (aged 0–4 years), and among adolescents and young adults (aged 15–29 years). The reasons for these 'peaks' in susceptibility can be explained, at least in part, by the method of spread of the bacteria that cause the disease. This is explained as follows.

Meningococcal disease is most common among young children, and among adolescents and young adults.

Meningococcal disease is caused by infection with bacteria called *Neisseria meningitides.* These bacteria live in the back of the throat of 'carriers' (about 20% of the population) and are spread to other people by various means. These include:

- kissing; and
- coughing or sneezing over a small child.

The bacteria are not spread as easily as some other bacteria and viruses that cause common respiratory illnesses. This is because *N. meningitides* is a large, heavy sort of bacteria. If a carrier sneezes or coughs in public, the bacteria are likely to fall quickly downwards—rather than being propelled into the mouths and noses of other people. They therefore usually die before they reach others. This is why meningococcal disease is not as contagious and common as other diseases—such as influenza for example. However, if there is a small child standing or lying below the carrier, the bacteria can fall onto the child and the child might thus contract meningococcal disease. This is one reason why small children are especially susceptible. In the case of adolescents, close physical contact (such as kissing) allows exchange of fluids (from the back of the throat) that contain the bacteria. This is one reason why adolescents are also at greater risk.

Common signs and symptoms

Because meningococcal disease is so difficult to diagnose and because children can rapidly become unwell (and perhaps die), it is very important that parents and carers know what to look for.

There are certain signs and symptoms that are commonly associated with meningococcal disease. These are listed in the Box below. Parents and carers should be aware that not all of these signs and symptoms are present in every case. In addition, they should know that most of these signs and symptoms can be present with other diseases. This makes diagnosis difficult.

Common signs and symptoms of meningococcal disease

In patients of any age

Certain signs and symptoms are commonly associated with meningococcal disease. However, not all of these signs and symptoms are present in every case.

- fever, pallor (paleness); rigours (shakes), sweats;
- headache, neck stiffness, photophobia (dislike of light); backache;
- vomiting and nausea, diarrhoea;
- lethargy (tiredness), drowsiness, irritability, confusion, agitation, seizures, altered conscious state;
- moaning, unintelligible speech;
- painful or swollen joints, myalgia (muscle pain); difficulty in walking; and
- haemorrhagic (blood-containing) rash—especially petechiae (purple-red or brownish spots) or purpura (collections of purple-red or brown skin discolouration).

In infants and young children

Additional signs and symptoms in infants and young children include:

- irritability, dislike of being handled;
- tiredness, floppiness, drowsiness;
- twitching or convulsions;
- grunting or moaning; and
- turning from light.

Typical rash

The most important sign of meningococcal disease listed in the Box is the characteristic rash. This is present in about 80% of cases. If the rash is present, the diagnosis is very likely to be meningococcal disease. However, if the rash is absent, this does not mean that the child does not have meningococcal disease.

If the rash is present, the diagnosis is very likely to be meningococcal disease; however, if the rash is absent, this does not mean that the child does not have the disease.

The rash is described as a 'haemorrhagic rash'. This means that it is a 'blood-containing' rash. It is purple-red or brownish in colour. It consists of petechiae (purple-red or brownish spots) or purpura (collections of purple-red or brown skin discolouration).

The rash can occur anywhere on the body. In many cases, especially early in the disease, the rash might be so slight that it is easily missed. In other cases it is widespread and obvious.

A useful test for the meningococcal rash is that it does not fade under pressure. One convenient way is to press on the rash with the side of a clear see-through drinking glass—to see through the glass how the rash responds. Most rashes from allergies or viral infections will fade, but the meningococcal rash does not usually fade (except in early stages of the disease).

Special warning signs

Apart from the common signs and symptoms listed in the Box on page 38, there are a few extra 'signs' that should especially alert parents and carers to potential 'trouble'. These additional signs are listed in the Box below. They are particularly applicable to staff at sick bays, surgeries, and hospitals.

Special warning signs

Apart from the common signs and symptoms of meningococcal disease, parents and carers should be aware that the following indicate potential 'trouble':

- rapid deterioration in child's condition;
- repeat presentations to surgery/sick bay/hospital; and
- expressions of special concern from child's parents or carers—particularly if these are usually calm and relaxed people.

These 'special' signs are listed here because meningococcal disease is difficult to diagnose. Even attentive and careful doctors and nurses can 'miss' the diagnosis in the early stages—especially if no rash is present. So parents and carers should always be alert to the signs listed in the Box. For example, if a child with meningococcal disease is sent home, but the child deteriorates rapidly (within a few hours), this should alert parents and carers to the possibility that a 'mistake' might have been made. They should take the child back for another urgent assessment. Similarly, if a child is brought back to a surgery or hospital soon after being sent home, it should be standard practice for the hospital to ensure that the child is seen by an experienced senior doctor. And if parents who are usually calm and collected appear to be especially worried, their concerns should be taken seriously. So-called 'gut feelings' are important. It is always better to be 'safe than sorry'.

"Gut feelings" are important; it is always better to be "safe than sorry".

Treatment

Meningococcal disease is obviously a serious, life-threatening condition—and urgent hospitalisation is required. The most important aspect of treatment is the immediate administration of antibiotics. In fact, most hospitals administer antibiotics to children if there is any suspicion of meningococcal disease—even if the diagnosis has not been 'officially' made.

Prophylactic (preventive) treatment is also recommended to all immediate close contacts—such as relatives, carers, and day-care contacts over the preceding 10 days.

Immunisation

Immunisation is now available for meningococcal disease. The vaccine protects against one of the two most common strains of bacteria responsible for meningococcal disease.

All children and adolescents should be immunised against meningococcal disease.

The availability of the vaccine varies from place to place. However, in Australia, the vaccine is now available free of charge to all children and adolescents from the age of 1 year to 19 years. All children and adolescents should be immunised against meningococcal disease.

Chapter 4

Coughs, Colds, Sneezes, and Wheezes

Causes of respiratory infections

Coughs, sneezes, and wheezes are all signs of various respiratory infections—that is, infections of the nose, throat, airways, and lungs. These infections can be caused by bacteria or viruses.

Although many people tend to think of viral infections as being less 'serious' than bacterial infections, this is not necessarily so. Many viral illnesses can be very serious. In addition, we have antibiotics to kill most bacteria. In contrast, anti-viral medications are only in the early stages of development and are not readily available to the general public (except in a few particular cases, such as for Herpes infections).

Framework of chapter

This chapter discusses conditions that cause 'coughs, colds, sneezes, and wheezes'. The chapter discusses the following subjects:

[*Note:* Asthma is discussed in a separate chapter. See Chapter 5, 'Asthma', page 55.]

Some common viruses that cause respiratory infections are:

- respiratory syncytial virus (RSV);
- influenza virus;
- parainfluenza virus; and
- rhinoviruses.

Some common bacteria that cause respiratory infections are:

- streptococci (various types);
- *Haemophilus influenzae* type B ('Hib');
- staphylococci, including *Staphylococcus aureus* ('golden staph'); and
- mycoplasma.

Common cold

Signs and symptoms

The 'common cold', as the name suggests, affects virtually everyone at some stage. It is usually caused by a rhinovirus.

The usual signs and symptoms are sore throat, stuffy nose, sneezing, nasal discharge, and cough. Other signs and symptoms include headache, muscular aches and pains, general malaise ('feeling generally unwell'), irritability, and lack of appetite.

Common cold and 'the flu'

Many people with these symptoms say that they have 'the flu' (by which they imply that they have influenza). However, in general, influenza is a more severe illness than the common cold. Most of the signs and symptoms—especially the general malaise (general 'unwellness')—are worse with influenza. Most people who have 'real influenza' (rather than a bad case of the common cold) simply cannot get out of bed to go to work or school.

There is usually no "runny nose" with influenza; a "runny nose" is a "good sign" that the infection is probably only a simple cold.

The one sign that is *not* more severe in influenza is the nasal discharge. There is usually no 'runny nose' with influenza. In fact, a runny nose is a 'good sign' that the infection is probably only a simple cold. If a child has other signs and symptoms of a cold (sore throat, stuffy nose, sneezing, and aches and pains), and if that child *also has a runny nose*, parents can be reasonably sure that the child has a common cold, rather than influenza.

So a nasal discharge is not a bad sign. In addition, parents and carers should also be aware that a *greenish* nasal discharge is not a bad sign. Nasal discharges in children often turn green after a while, and this does *not* necessarily mean that the child has a secondary bacterial infection that requires antibiotics.

Treatment

Treatment for the common cold is *symptomatic*—that is, treatment is aimed at controlling the worst effects of the symptoms, rather than trying to remove the cause. Such symptomatic treatment

Technical terms used in this chapter

This chapter uses some technical terms as a 'shorthand' way of describing what happens in certain illnesses. Most of these are explained in the text, but this list might also be helpful.

Antibiotics
Medications that kill bacteria

Exhalation/exhaling
Breathing out

Incubation period
The time from when a child gets an infection until he or she becomes unwell

Inhalation/inhaling
Breathing in

Lower respiratory tract infections
Infections in the lower part of the lungs

Microbe
Microscopic organisms that can cause disease (mainly bacteria or viruses)

Sign
Something that a parent or carer notices in a sick child (such as a rash)

Stridor
A loud noise that indicates obstruction to breathing; heard when a child is *inhaling* (breathing in)

Symptomatic treatment
Treatment that aims to relieve symptoms (such as itch or pain) without attempting to cure the cause

Symptom
Something that the sick child complains about but other people cannot see (such as pain)

Susceptible
People who might get an infectious disease because they have not had it before, or because they have not had an immunisation, or because they have some other medical problem

Upper respiratory tract infections
Infections in the nose, throat, and upper airways (top part of the lungs)

Wheeze
A noise that indicates obstruction to breathing; heard when a child is *exhaling* (breathing out)

might include medications to dry up the secretions or diminish the cough. There is no specific treatment to kill the virus itself.

Parents and carers should be aware that children who have had a cold can continue to cough for a week or two after other symptoms have gone. If the cough continues any longer than a few weeks, they should seek a medical opinion.

Bronchiolitis

What is bronchiolitis?

Bronchiolitis is a respiratory disease of very young children. The vast majority of cases occur in children under 12 months of age.

Most parents and carers will have heard of 'bronchitis'. This means 'inflammation of the bronchi'—the large airways of the lungs. Similarly, the term 'bronchiolitis' refers to inflammation of airways, but in this case it describes 'inflammation of the *bronchioles*' (rather than bronchi). The bronchioles are small airways fairly deep in the lungs. Bronchiolitis is therefore called a *lower* respiratory tract infection (as opposed to an *upper* respiratory tract infection).

Bronchiolitis is the most common lower respiratory tract infection in infants and young children.

Bronchiolitis is the most common lower respiratory tract infection in infants and young children. In fact, about 40% of all children have at least one episode (although most are mild and not serious). About 1% of all infants require hospitalisation for bronchiolitis. Most cases occur in winter in temperate climates, or in the 'rainy season' in tropical climates.

Cause

Almost all cases of bronchiolitis are caused by the respiratory syncytial virus (RSV). This virus is a common cause of respiratory infection in children. It is also responsible for some cases of croup and pneumonia.

Natural immunity to the virus is slow to develop, and is incomplete. Repeat attacks can occur. There is a vaccine available, but it is very expensive and is usually given only to low birthweight babies.

RSV is unusual in that it can live for relatively long periods of time outside the human body. Most other viruses die relatively quickly after they are coughed or sneezed from the lungs and throat, but RSV can live for several hours on the hands of people (including parents and carers), on household surfaces (such as cots and tables), and on toys touched by an infected child. It is therefore important to separate children who have bronchiolitis from other children—with the child's cot being at least six feet away from another child's bed or cot. In addition, steps should be taken to prevent the RSV virus being picked up on hands or objects, and then carried to another child. All carers should wash their hands carefully after touching the child, and the walls and surfaces around the cot should be carefully wiped down with hot water and and detergent regularly. If a disinfectant is used, it should be applied only after cleaning with detergent. Disinfectants should always be made up (and used) strictly according to the manufacturer's instructions.

The aim is to prevent the RSV virus being picked up on hands or objects, and then carried to another child.

Signs and symptoms

Bronchiolitis begins with a fever, runny nose, and dry cough. This usually proceeds fairly quickly to increasing breathlessness and wheeze (an audible 'tight' sound as the child breathes out). In many cases, bronchiolitis can be difficult to distinguish from asthma.

In severe cases, the breathing difficulties can become quite marked, and the child can have problems in eating and drinking. Medical attention is certainly required by this stage—for both the breathing problems and the problems that come with a lack of intake of fluids. In a small number of cases, bronchiolitis can be fatal.

It is therefore important that parents and carers carefully observe any child with bronchiolitis. The child should be taken to hospital immediately if there are signs of distress. The signs in the Box below indicate that the child is in significant difficulty (and probably should already be in hospital).

It is important that parents carefully observe any child with bronchiolitis. The child should be taken to hospital immediately if there are signs of distress.

Signs of concern in bronchiolitis

A child with bronchiolitis should be taken to hospital immediately if there are signs of distress. The following signs indicate that the child is in significant difficulty (and probably should already be in hospital):

- rapid breathing (50–100 breaths per minute);
- a rapid heart rate (140–200 beats per minute);
- a worsening cough (usually sharp and dry);
- chest movements that indicate the child is obviously working hard to breathe;
- audible 'crackles and wheezes' when breathing;
- pale or bluish colour to face and limbs; and
- periods of not breathing and turning blue.

Treatment

There is no specific treatment for the infection. In fact, there is not a lot that parents and carers can actually do—apart from watching carefully and seeking immediate medical attention if the child deteriorates. The child should be handled as little as possible; it is better not to disturb the child unnecessarily.

In hospital, treatment is aimed at supporting the child's breathing and ensuring adequate fluid intake.

Pneumonia

Causes

The term 'pneumonia' refers to a deep-seated infection of the delicate lung tissue where oxygen is absorbed. There are many types of pneumonia and a variety of bacteria and viruses can cause it. Most cases are caused by viruses.

Pneumonia often comes after a respiratory infection—such as a cold or the 'flu'. Most children with pneumonia can be managed at home and get better quite quickly and completely.

Signs and symptoms

In general, a combination of a high fever and breathing difficulties indicates that pneumonia is present.

The typical pattern of onset is sudden. Over a relatively short time (often less than 24 hours), the child develops a high fever, cough, difficulties with breathing, and rigours (muscle spasms). Older children might also begin to cough up foul-coloured phlegm. Younger children might also be producing this phlegm, but parents do not see it because the child either cannot cough it up or swallows it.

In general, a combination of a high fever and breathing difficulties indicates that pneumonia is present.

The child looks unwell and has a fast breathing rate and a fast heart rate. Many children develop a typical breathing 'grunt'. This is a repetitive, low-pitched, grunting noise at the end of each breath out. This is more typical of younger children than older children.

Children with pneumonia usually do not drink well, and parents and carers should watch fluid intake carefully.

Treatment

Because it is difficult to tell whether pneumonia is caused by bacteria or viruses, antibiotics (to kill bacteria) are usually prescribed. If parents or carers suspect pneumonia in a child, they should therefore seek medical attention with a view to obtaining antibiotics if the diagnosis is confirmed. In most cases, antibiotics will be prescribed if there is any likelihood of pneumonia being present.

Apart from giving antibiotics, parents and carers should ensure the child rests and has adequate fluid intake. Cough medicines should not be given to children with pneumonia. Medical assistance should be sought if the child is becoming increasingly distressed.

Mycoplasma

What is mycoplasma?

Most parents and carers would not have heard of a microbe called 'mycoplasma', but it is surprisingly common. Mycoplasma is a bacteria-like microbe that causes a number of mild-to-moderate respiratory illnesses in children. These can vary from upper respiratory infections (usually in younger children) to lower respiratory infections (usually in children older than five years of age). Many cases are not actually diagnosed as being due to mycoplasma.

Mycoplasma causes a number of mild-to-moderate respiratory illnesses in children ... Many cases are not actually diagnosed as being due to mycoplasma.

The disease is typically spread within families. Often two or more siblings will develop respiratory infections. Sometimes a parent can develop an infection. The incubation period is about three weeks.

Younger children

In pre-school children, mycoplasma typically causes upper respiratory tract infections. These usually cause a runny nose and sore throat. In some cases they can progress to the lower respiratory tract and lead to bronchitis—which causes a cough.

Older children

In children aged more than five years, mycoplasma can cause a mild-to-moderate form of pneumonia. This is not usually as severe as 'classical' bacterial pneumonia (see page 45). The child does not usually develop a high temperature and breathing difficulties. Indeed, the diagnosis is usually made after some time when a child is taken to the doctor because he or she takes 'too long' to get better after an apparently mild respiratory infection. The illness never seems to be especially severe, but it just won't go away!

Treatment

Because mycoplasma behaves like bacteria in many respects, it can be killed with antibiotics. However, many children get better on their own without any specific treatment.

Croup

What is croup?

Croup is not a 'single disease' caused by a 'single virus'. Croup is more about a particular child's *reaction to an infection*, rather than the precise nature of the infection itself. It is more common in young children (aged six months to three years), with a peak incidence at about two years of age.

Croup is a significant narrowing of the upper airways (around the throat and voice box). It occurs when the (already narrow) upper airways of a small child become even more narrow and obstructed as a result of swelling in the lining of the airways. This obstruction produces a characteristic breathing noise called a 'stridor'.

Obstruction produces a characteristic breathing noise called a "stridor".

A 'stridor' is a harsh, loud noise made when the child is inhaling (breathing in). A stridor is therefore different from a wheeze. A wheeze occurs when a child is *exhaling* (breathing out), whereas a stridor occurs when the child is *inhaling* (breathing in).

A number of different viruses can cause swelling of the upper airways in susceptible children. These include influenza viruses, parainfluenza viruses, adenoviruses, rhinoviruses, and RSV (the virus that causes bronchiolitis, see page 44). Because there is such a wide variety of viruses that can produce the condition, and because the reaction depends on the reaction of a particular child's body (rather than a specific infection), there is no immunisation available against croup.

Signs and symptoms

Mild croup

Mild croup usually begins with a slight fever for 1–2 days. The child often develops a hoarse voice. This is followed by a cough (a loud persistent 'barking cough') and the development of a stridor (a harsh, loud noise made when the child is breathing in).

The stridor typically develops at night, and parents can be understandably frightened when a small child suddenly develops a barking cough and a loud breathing noise (stridor) in the middle of the night. However, the condition usually sounds worse than it really is (see below, page 48, for signs of 'Severe croup').

In many cases, this pattern goes on for several nights in a row. However, after 2–3 days the condition usually settles down and goes away by about 7 days.

Severe croup

Severe croup follows a similar pattern, but the child becomes much worse. The signs of severe croup are listed in the Box below. If a child with croup develops any of these signs, an urgent trip to hospital is required.

Treatment

The most important aspect of treatment at home is a cuddle! This might seem trivial, but it is *extremely important* to relieve the child's anxiety. If the child becomes very upset (and remains very upset), this will make the swelling in the throat worse. If a child develops croup in the middle of the night, it is therefore very important that parents lift the child from his or her bed or cot, sit the child upright on their laps, and provide a cuddle and reassuring, soothing words to relax the child as much as possible.

It is also worth trying 'steam treatment'. This does not work in every case, but warm, moist air does seem to help some children with an attack of croup. The shower can be turned on 'hot' in the bathroom, and the child can then be carried into the steamed-up bathroom for a reassuring cuddle with a parent (while both are sitting on a chair in the middle of the room). If the stridor does not ease within about 10 minutes the child should be taken to hospital. It might be necessary to call an ambulance.

Apart from reassuring cuddles and steam, the child should be interfered with as little as possible. Nothing should be done that causes the child more anxiety or distress. This will only make the croup worse. There is no need to check the child's temperature—especially if this causes the child more distress. No attempt should be made to look down the child's throat.

If the child does not get better (or indeed becomes worse), the child should be taken to a hospital for assessment and treatment.

Signs of severe croup

If a child with croup develops any of the following signs, an urgent trip to hospital is required:

- pallor (pale skin) and weakness;
- increasing difficulty in breathing ('working hard' to breathe);
- fast breathing rate and fast heart rate;
- restlessness; and
- blue lips or fingers.

Epiglottitis

What is epiglottitis?

The epiglottis is a little movable flap of tissue in the throat. It moves up and down as required when people are speaking and/or eating. It thus protects the larynx (and airways) from food and other material going down into the lungs.

Epiglottitis is inflammation of this little flap of tissue in the throat—caused by a bacterial infection. It can rapidly cause obstruction to the child's airway. Epiglottitis is therefore a very serious, life-threatening illness; urgent referral to a hospital is required. However, the disease is relatively uncommon—especially since immunisation against *Haemophilus influenzae* type B ('Hib') has been introduced.

Signs and symptoms

Epiglottitis can occur at any age (including adults). However, the peak age in children is about 2–3 years.

Because epiglottitis can be rapidly life-threatening, it is obviously important that parents and carers know how to recognise the condition. In many ways, it is similar to croup—except the child is usually much sicker with epiglottitis. This is because the infection is caused by a serious bacterial infection that also causes 'blood poisoning'. So, in addition to local inflammation in the throat (causing breathing difficulties, as in croup), a child with epiglottitis is usually very unwell and 'toxic'.

A useful acronym for parents and carers to learn is 'SNORED'. The letters stand for the first letters of the following signs and symptoms:

- Septic and Sitting upright
- NO cough
- Rapid onset
- Expiratory snore
- Drooling

Each of these is discussed below. However, it should be noted that *not all* cases of epiglottitis have *all* of the signs. The acronym 'SNORED' is useful to remember, but parents and carers should *not* assume that all cases of epiglottitis fit the pattern exactly.

The acronym 'SNORED' is useful to remember, but parents and carers should *not* assume that all cases of epiglottitis fit the pattern exactly.

Septic and Sitting upright

As discussed above, a child with epiglottitis is usually very unwell and 'toxic'. The child usually has a high fever and 'looks sick'.

In addition, older children often want to sit upright. This is because an upright posture makes it easier to breathe past the inflamed epiglottis. Younger children (especially infants) will remain lying down, but they often lie on their front with their bottoms in the air—again because this helps them to breathe more easily.

No cough

This sign should not be taken too literally; some children with epiglottitis *do* have a cough. However, as a general 'rule of thumb', a basic difference between croup and epiglottitis is that children with croup nearly always have a cough whereas children with epiglottitis usually do not.

Rapid onset

Children with epiglottitis become very unwell very quickly. They go from being (apparently) perfectly well to being very unwell within 2–6 hours.

'SNORED'

In remembering the signs and symptoms of epiglottitis, a useful acronym for parents and carers to learn is 'SNORED'. The letters stand for the first letters of the following signs and symptoms:

- Septic and Sitting upright
- NO cough
- Rapid onset
- Expiratory snore
- Drooling

Expiratory snore

Children with epiglottitis develop a characteristic snoring sound when they breathe out. Unlike croup (which has an *inspiratory* stridor on breathing in), children with epiglottitis develop a distinctive 'snoring noise' (much like an adult snoring softly) at the end of each breath out.

Drooling

Children with epiglottitis often have saliva drooling from their mouths. This is because the blockage in their throat prevents them from swallowing in the normal manner.

Treatment

The main principles of treatment are:

- seek expert medical and nursing attention as soon as possible; and
- interfere as little as possible.

Children with epiglottitis have a very narrow airway, and *any* upset could lead to the airway being suddenly cut off. It is therefore very important that parents and carers do not 'interfere' with the child unnecessarily. They should remain calm, comfort the child, and get to expert medical help as soon as possible. In particular, it is important that carers do not attempt to look in the child's mouth or throat, or take the child's temperature, or remove the child from a comfortable seated position with a caring adult.

It is very important that parents and carers do not 'interfere' with the child unnecessarily; they should remain calm, comfort the child, and get to expert medical help as soon as possible.

Children with epiglottitis are usually transported from doctors' clinics or general hospitals to a major paediatric hospital using an expert paediatric transport service. They are then treated with antibiotics and other life-saving resuscitation procedures (if required).

The case of Tom (see Box, page 51) is a good example of how a case of epiglottitis should be handled.

Hib immunisation

All children should be immunised against *Haemophilus influenzae* type B (Hib) as part of their infant immunisation program. Hib is one of the major causes of epiglottitis. Immunisation does

Tom

Tom was a little boy who was apparently well when he was dropped off at pre-school by his father. Two hours later, Tom's father was telephoned by staff asking him to come urgently to pick up the little boy and take him to hospital.

In that brief period of two hours, Tom had become very unwell and was having trouble breathing. His father returned to the pre-school and took him to hospital immediately.

When the nursing staff assessed Tom in hospital, they found him sitting up on his father's knee and leaning forward. He was hot and 'toxic'. When he breathed out he made a soft 'snoring' noise. And he was drooling from the mouth.

The nurses assessed that Tom was probably suffering from epiglottitis. They therefore made no attempt to interfere with the little boy in any way—because they did not want to cause Tom any distress and thus put his breathing in jeopardy. The nurses did not attempt to look in his mouth or throat. Nor did they attempt to take his temperature, or try to give him oxygen. They simply left him sitting quietly on his father's knee and observed him from a distance while they contacted an emergency paediatric transport service.

Tom made a complete recovery from his epiglottitis. Everyone had played their part appropriately. The pre-school staff had recognised that something was seriously wrong and had called the little boy's father immediately. Tom's father had responded promptly and had provided his son with comfort and reassurance. The nursing staff had correctly diagnosed the problem, and had not interfered in any way that might cause the little boy alarm and anxiety. Tom was taken to a major paediatric hospital by an expert transport team. He was treated appropriately at every stage.

not mean that a child cannot get epiglottitis from another sort of bacteria, but it does decrease the risks considerably.

Whooping cough

What is whooping cough?

Whooping cough (also called 'pertussis') is a bacterial infection of the upper respiratory tract caused by bacteria called *Bordetella pertussis.* It occurs in epidemics and affects people of all ages (including adults), but is most dangerous in infants and small children. The most prominent feature of whooping cough is a persistent, annoying, debilitating cough—which can go on for months.

Phases in illness

A typical case of whooping cough has three stages:

- catarrhal ('runny nose') stage;
- paroxysmal ('bursts of coughing') stage; and
- convalescent ('recovery') stage.

Each of these is discussed below.

Catarrhal ('runny nose') stage

The first stage lasts for several days or a week, and resembles a common cold. The child has a runny nose, a sore throat, and a mild temperature. There is no indication at this stage that the illness might be whooping cough.

Paroxysmal ('bursts of coughing') stage

In this stage the child develops paroxysms of coughing (or 'bursts' of coughing). In a 'classic case' of whooping cough, the child develops episodes of severe, repetitive coughing, and 'whooping'. There is a distinctive pattern to each paroxysm of coughing. The pattern consists of a number of severe repeated coughs on *each exhalation* ('breath out'), followed by a longish 'whoop' on the *next inhalation* (breath in). The sequence goes like this:

[breath out] ... 'cough' ... 'cough' ... 'cough' ... 'cough' ... 'cough'

followed by:

[breath in] ... 'whooooop' ...

The sequence is then repeated. This can go on and on, sometimes for several minutes at a time—thus leaving the child exhausted. Episodes of vomiting can follow a paroxysm of coughing. Between the paroxysms of coughing and whooping, the child can appear to be quite well.

The important characteristic of the cough in 'classical' whooping cough is a series of repeated 'rapid-fire' coughs on a single exhalation (breath out).

The important characteristic of the cough in "classical" whooping cough is a series of repeated "rapid-fire" coughs on a single exhalation.

This is the 'classic case', and if it occurs as described above the diagnosis is fairly easy to make. However, in many cases, the pattern is less clear. For example, infants do not usually 'whoop'; and older children whoop less often than pre-school children. In addition, the pattern of the paroxysms of coughing (bursts of coughing) can vary. In some cases the child is just thought to have an annoying persistent cough that won't go away.

This phase can go on for weeks, or even months.

Convalescent ('recovery') stage

The convalescent (or 'recovery') stage lasts for 1–2 weeks. In this stage there is a decrease in the severity and frequency of the cough, and the child gradually begins to feel better. However, the cough can continue (on and off) for several months, and any new upper respiratory infection can bring the cough back again.

Complications

Whooping cough can be a serious disease. Apart from the illness itself—which can be quite exhausting and debilitating—there are certain complications that can develop. These include the following.

- *Respiratory arrest:* In infants, a small plug of mucus can lodge in an airway during a paroxysm of coughing. Because infants have such small airways, this can cause blockage of the airway. Respiratory arrest (no breathing) can occur. Infants and very small children can thus die from whooping cough.
- *Pneumonia:* Some children can develop bacterial pneumonia as a result of whooping cough. Although this complication is not as sudden and dramatic as respiratory arrest, it can be life-threatening.

- *Encephalitis:* Infection of the brain can occur with whooping cough. This usually produces seizures or coma.

Whooping cough is therefore, potentially, a very serious disease—especially in infants and small children. Because the disease is sometimes difficult to diagnose, and is often difficult to treat (see below, this page), it is therefore important that it be prevented, if possible, by immunisation.

Immunisation

Immunisation against whooping cough (pertussis) is usually provided as part of routine infant immunisations. However, immunisation is not always effective, and it certainly does not provide 100% immunity for life.

Whooping cough can sometimes occur in a fully immunised child. In addition, 95% of people who are immunised are susceptible again after 12 years. In other words, the immunisation 'wears off'.

Despite these problems, it is certainly worthwhile having immunisation. The overwhelming majority (70%) of children who are *not* immunised will get whooping cough.

All children (especially infants and young children) should be immunised against whooping cough.

All children (especially infants and young children) should therefore be immunised against whooping cough—even children who have previously had the disease.

Adolescents and adults working with young children or planning to become parents, should receive a booster dose of whooping cough (pertussis) vaccine.

Treatment

If the diagnosis is clearcut, the child might be admitted to hospital or might be treated at home. Hospital admission should be seriously considered in any child under six months of age.

The *Bordetella pertussis* bacteria that cause whooping cough are killed by an antibiotic called erythromycin. This is the only antibiotic that will work. Although it is a commonly used antibiotic in many respiratory infections, erythromycin is not the *only* commonly used antibiotic. This can cause problems if the diagnosis is unclear. For example, if a child has a persistent annoying cough, several different antibiotics might be tried before erythromycin is tried. It is a good idea for parents and carers (and doctors) to keep whooping cough in mind as a possible diagnosis in all cases of persistent annoying cough that does not clear up as expected with other treatment.

Cough mixtures are of no use in whooping cough. The cough is the most distressing symptom, but unfortunately there is no specific treatment for it.

Once erythromycin is started, the child is no longer infectious, and the child gradually begins to get better. However, the coughing paroxysms can still continue for some weeks. The antibiotic should also be given to other family members (including adults).

Once erythromycin is started, the child is no longer infectious, and the child gradually begins to get better; however, the coughing paroxysms can still continue for some weeks.

Chapter 5

Asthma

A common problem

Asthma affects a significant proportion of the population. For example, in Australia, asthma affects:

- approximately 2 in every 5 children;
- approximately 1 in 7 teenagers; and
- approximately 1 in 10 adults.

In addition, the incidence of asthma appears to be increasing. It is unclear exactly why this is so. Asthma appears to be an illness of developed societies. It is also possible that asthma is being diagnosed more often.

Framework of chapter

This chapter discusses asthma under the following headings:

Risk factors for asthma

For individuals, there are certain risk factors that increase the likelihood of developing asthma. A child is more likely to develop asthma if that child:

- has atopy (an allergic tendency) at an early age—for example: hives, eczema, hayfever;
- has one or both parents who have asthma;
- is exposed to tobacco smoke in utero (during mother's pregnancy) or in first two years of life; and
- has a serious respiratory illness (one that requires hospital treatment) before two years of age.

Trigger factors for asthma

A child who has an asthmatic tendency is more likely to have an asthma episode in certain circumstances. These vary from child to child, but can include:

- viral respiratory tract infections—such as the common cold; this is certainly the most common trigger factor in small children;
- allergens—such as pollen and dust mites;
- exercise—although children with asthma should not be discouraged from exercising; these children need better control of their asthma, not less exercise;
- irritants—certain chemicals in the air;
- temperature changes—especially sudden decreases in temperature (for example, a 10-degree drop in temperature with a sudden cool change);
- occupational triggers;
- certain medications; and
- emotional upset.

These trigger factors differ from child to child, and each case has to be considered on its merits. However, a few general points can be made about some of the 'preventable' trigger factors.

Viral respiratory tract infections

Viral infections are the most common 'trigger' for asthma episodes in children. It is almost impossible to prevent children coming into contact with such diseases, and asthmatic children should not be isolated from other children. However, reasonable measures should be taken to prevent asthmatic children coming into contact with people who are *known* to have an infectious disease. In addition, adjustments to the child's treatment plan might be needed at the first sign of any viral infection. (For more on management plans, see 'Management', page 61.)

Viral infections are the most common 'trigger' for asthma episodes in children.

Allergens

If a child is known to be allergic to dust mites, there is usually no need to take extreme measures—such as pulling up all the carpets in a house. Dust mites don't fly and they don't jump! A simple measure such as preventing an allergic child from lying on the carpet is likely to be just as effective as removing all the carpets in the house. In addition, the fitting of a proper mattress cover (preferably one approved by health authorities) is recommended.

Technical terms used in this chapter

This chapter uses some technical terms as a 'shorthand' way of describing what happens in asthma. Most of these are explained in the text, but this list might also be helpful.

Acute

Recent, sudden, short-lived; (note that 'acute' does not necessarily mean 'severe'; rather, 'acute' refers to the *time-span* involved; it is the opposite of 'chronic')

Allergen

Something in the environment (for example, pollen) that triggers an allergic reaction in certain people

Atopy

Allergic tendency (for example: hives, eczema, hayfever)

Bronchodilator

A medication that relaxes the airways and opens up the lungs; (sometimes called 'reliever medication', as opposed to 'preventive medication')

Chronic

Long-term

Exhalation/exhaling

Breathing out

Inhalation/inhaling

Breathing in

Management

An overall plan of treatment and prevention

Preventive medication

Medication that aims to prevent episodes of asthma occurring

Reliever medication

A bronchodilator; a medication that relaxes the airways and opens up the lungs (a 'treatment' medication, as opposed to 'preventive' medication)

Sign

Something that a parent or carer notices in a sick child (such as a rash)

Symptom

Something that the sick child complains about but other people cannot see (such as pain)

Upper respiratory tract infections

Infections in the nose, throat, and upper airways (top part of the lungs)

Wheeze

A noise that indicates obstruction to breathing; heard when a child is *exhaling* (breathing out)

Exercise

Children who have exercise-induced asthma should not be stopped from exercising. Rather, their asthma management should be tailored to allow them to exercise regularly and safely.

Children with exercise-induced asthma should not be stopped from exercising; their asthma management should be tailored to allow them to exercise.

They should take a dose of their 'reliever' medication 5–10 minutes before exercising, and further doses if they develop symptoms. Their 'reliever' medication should always be on hand for immediate use if required. (For more on types of medications, see 'Management', page 61.)

Children who suffer from exercise-induced asthma should also do a proper warm-up routine, and try to breathe through their noses when exercising.

Occupational triggers

In assessing possible triggers for asthma in children, the occupation and habits of parents should be taken into account. Some children react to exposure to chemicals or dust brought home from work by a parent. The story of Mary (Box, below) provides an example.

Mary

Mary suffered from repeated asthma episodes in the mornings. Her parents could not find a 'trigger' for these episodes, and eventually they decided that it was just a 'morning thing'.

Some time later they were discussing the issue again, and they realised that the episodes always occurred soon after Mary's father arrived home from his early-morning work at a bakery. Following up on this idea, they discovered that Mary was allergic to flour dust brought home on her father's clothes.

The problem was solved by arranging for Mary's father to shower and change his clothes before coming into contact with his daughter.

Medications

Almost any medication can cause an allergic reaction in a susceptible individual, and asthmatic children do have a tendency to such allergic reactions. It is therefore difficult to be confident about which medications should be given to asthmatic children and which should not. However, as a general rule, aspirin and ibuprofen are usually not given to asthmatic children—because these medications have been found to be 'triggers' in some cases.

Signs and symptoms

The characteristic 'wheeze' is the most important sign of asthma. A wheeze is a noise that indicates obstruction to breathing. It is heard when a child is *exhaling* (breathing out).

Other signs and symptoms include:

- chest tightness;
- shortness of breath; and
- cough.

This combination of signs and symptoms (wheeze, chest tightness, shortness of breath, and cough) is characteristic of asthma—especially if they occur after a typical triggering event (such as exercise, exposure to irritants or allergens, or viral infections).

A chronic (long-term) cough at night can be the only sign. However, this is rare. It is much more common for one or more of the other signs and symptoms (wheeze, chest tightness, shortness of breath) to be also present.

Wheeze, chest tightness, shortness of breath, and cough are characteristic of asthma—especially if they occur after a typical triggering event.

Diagnosis

If a child has the signs and symptoms listed above, the diagnosis is likely to be asthma. This is especially likely if the child has a history of allergic problems (for example: eczema, hives) or if there is a family history of asthma in a close relative.

The diagnosis is confirmed by testing the child's response to asthma medication. The usual medication that is used is an inhaled bronchodilator—a medication that relaxes the airways and opens up the lungs (sometimes called a 'reliever' medication). If the child's signs and symptoms go away after inhaling a bronchodilator (such as 'Ventolin'), the diagnosis is asthma. To put it simply: asthma responds to anti-asthma medications; if it doesn't respond, it's not asthma.

Asthma responds to anti-asthma medications; if it doesn't respond, it's not asthma.

Patterns of asthma

There are three broad patterns of asthma. Although some children do not fit neatly into one of these categories, the three broad patterns are useful for planning overall treatment (or management) of asthma. The three patterns are:

- infrequent episodic asthma;
- frequent episodic asthma; and
- persistent asthma.

Each of these is discussed below.

Infrequent episodic asthma

As the name suggests, this pattern of asthma involves isolated episodes of asthma that do not occur very often. This category includes about 70–75% of all children with asthma.

With infrequent episodic asthma, the episodes of asthma are usually more than 6–8 weeks apart. The child is well between episodes. Each episode lasts a variable time—from a day or two to a week or two. The episodes are usually triggered by an upper respiratory tract infection or an environmental allergen.

Most cases of infrequent episodic asthma are mild, although severe episodes *can* occur from time to time.

Most children with this pattern of asthma tend to improve as they become older. About two-thirds will cease having episodes of asthma by the time they are adults (or have only very infrequent, very mild episodes). However, it is not wise to say that an individual has 'grown out' of asthma completely. Some people do suffer recurrent episodes of asthma later in life (for example, at the age of 40 years or so). Nevertheless, the outlook for this group is generally good.

Children with infrequent episodic asthma do not usually require preventive medication.

Management (treatment) for this group involves bronchodilators ('relievers'). only. Children with infrequent episodic asthma do not usually require preventive medication. (For more on management of asthma, see 'Management', page 61.)

Patterns of asthma

This part of the chapter discusses three patterns of asthma. These can be summarised as follows.

Infrequent episodic asthma

- isolated episodes of asthma that do not occur very often
- child is well in interval period between episodes
- about 70–75% of all children with asthma

Frequent episodic asthma

- isolated episodes of asthma that do occur often
- child is well in interval period between episodes
- about 20% of all children with asthma

Persistent asthma

- acute episodes of asthma (like the other two patterns)
- these children *also* have signs and symptoms of asthma on most days in the interval period between episodes
- about 5–10% of all children with asthma

Frequent episodic asthma

The second pattern of asthma involves more frequent episodes than the first. This category includes about 20% of all children with asthma.

In the *frequent* episodic category, the interval between the episodes of asthma is less than in the *infrequent* group—that is, the interval is less than 6–8 weeks. Like the *infrequent* group, each episode of asthma lasts from a day or two to a week or two. The child is well between episodes.

Children with frequent episodic asthma might need preventive medication.

Because children with frequent episodic asthma are having asthma more often, they might need preventive medication (as well as bronchodilators). (For more on management of asthma, see 'Management', page 61.)

Persistent asthma

The third pattern of asthma also involves acute episodes of asthma (like the other two patterns), but the difference with this persistent group lies in the interval period. These children *also* have signs and symptoms of asthma on most days in the interval period between episodes. This category includes about 5–10% of all children with asthma.

Because children with persistent asthma are having asthma more often *and also* having signs and symptoms of asthma between episodes, they *do* need preventive medication (as well as bronchodilators). (For more on management of asthma, see 'Management', page 61.)

Children with persistent asthma *do* need preventive medication.

Management

Aims of management

It is better to think about the 'management' of asthma, rather than the 'treatment' of asthma. The term 'management' refers to an overall plan for the long-term treatment and prevention of asthma.

Because asthma cannot be cured, the aims of management are to control the condition as well as possible. The aims of asthma management can be summarised as follows:

- to achieve best quality of life by minimising symptoms and maintaining best lung function;
- to minimise absence from school or work;
- to identify triggers and prevent children being exposed to them as much as possible;
- to minimise the risk of death from an acute episode (most likely in older children aged 11–14 years, but can occur at any age).

Management plan

All children who have asthma should have an individualised asthma management plan. This should include:

- a list of regular medications and dosages;
- how to recognise a worsening of the condition; and
- when, where, and how to get urgent assistance.

The plan should be developed in conjunction with a general practitioner, and should be reviewed every six months.

Types of medication

The three main types of asthma medications are:

- relievers;
- symptom controllers; and
- preventers.

Each of these is discussed below.

Relievers

'Relievers' are medications that open up the airways. Their technical name is 'bronchodilators'. They are usually inhaled (from a 'puffer'), although they can be given by injection.

Management of asthma

This part of the chapter discusses the management of asthma. The following subjects are discussed.

These medications work by relaxing the tight muscles in the airways, and are used as required to relieve episodes of asthma. They do not reduce inflammation (as 'preventers' do).

Some common fast-acting 'relievers' are:

- salbutamol ('Ventolin', 'Respolin', 'Respax', 'Asmol', 'Airomir');
- terbutaline ('Bricanyl'); and
- fenoterol ('Berotec').

A slower-acting 'reliever' is:

- ipratropium ('Atrovent', 'Combivent').

Symptom controllers

Symptom controllers are also bronchodilators (similar to 'relievers'); however, they work more slowly and for a longer time. They are taken, by inhalation from a 'puffer', at certain prescribed times during the day—rather than 'as required'.

The main use of these medications is to keep signs and symptoms under control over a prolonged period of 6–12 hours. They are especially useful overnight and for combating exercise-induced asthma. They should not be used to treat an acute episode; they do not work quickly enough.

Some common 'symptom controllers' are:

- salmeterol ('Serevent'); and
- eformoterol ('Foradile', 'Oxis')

Preventers

'Preventers' are not bronchodilators (like 'relievers' and 'symptom controllers'); rather they are anti-inflammatories. 'Preventers' are therefore *not* used to treat acute episodes of asthma; rather, they are used to decrease allergic inflammation in the airways and thus prevent episodes of asthma.

Preventers are used to prevent episodes of asthma.

They are slow-acting medications and must be taken every day as directed. They can take 2–4 weeks to have an effect.

Some children need to take them all-year round. Others need to use them only at particular times of the year (such as spring and summer). However, if they are not being used all-year round, it is important to know that they take a few weeks to begin working and that they must be used every day to get a proper effect.

Some common antihistamine-type 'preventers' are:

- sodium cromoglycate ('Intal'); and
- nedocromil sodium ('Tilade').

Some common steroid-type 'preventers' are:

- beclomethasone ('Aldecin', 'Becotide', 'Becloforte', 'Respocort');
- budesonide ('Pulmicort'); and
- fluticasone ('Flixotide').

Newer medications (available in chewable tablet form) are known as:

- leukotriene-receptor antagonists (LTRAs)—such as montelukast ('Singulair').

First-aid plan

The medications described above are used in various combinations, according to the child's pattern of asthma. It is impossible to list every possible combination. This should be discussed with a doctor as part of an individualised management plan. However, it is possible to give advice on an emergency first-aid plan of action if a child becomes rapidly unwell with an asthma attack. The Box below provides a simple 4-step plan that every parent or carer should know.

Four-step asthma first-aid plan

Step 1

- Sit the child up.
- Be calm and reassuring.

Step 2

- Without delay, give 4 separate puffs of the child's 'reliever' medication.
- Give one puff at a time via a spacer.
- Ask the child to breathe in and out 4 times after each puff.

Step 3

- Wait 4 minutes.

Step 4

- If there is no improvement, repeat steps 2 and 3.
- If still no improvement, ring for an ambulance.
- Continue to repeat steps 2 and 3 while waiting for the ambulance.

Spacers

What is a spacer?

Many parents and carers will be familiar with 'spacers'. These are clear, plastic cylinders of various shapes with an opening at each end. A medication 'puffer' is placed at one end, and the other end has a mouthpiece or mask for the child to use. A dose of medication is 'puffed' into the spacer and the child then inhales through the mouthpiece or mask at the other end.

There are various sizes and shapes of spacers.

- For children under three years of age, a small spacer with a mask is recommended.
- For children aged three years to six years, a small spacer with a mouthpiece is recommended.
- For children aged six years and older, a large spacer with a mouthpiece is recommended.

Using a spacer

In using a puffer and spacer, it is important to administer one puff into the spacer at a time. The child then takes 4–5 breaths from the other end of the spacer—breathing in and out normally. There is no need to take rapid breaths or very deep breaths.

The number of doses ('puffs') administered at each 'sitting' depends on the dose prescribed by the doctor. However, if the child receives three or more 'puffs' at a 'sitting', the puffer should be removed from the spacer and shaken a few times before being replaced in the spacer and used again.

Advantages of a spacer

Spacers were originally introduced to assist children (especially smaller children) with the problem of coordinating their inhalation (breath in) with the use of a 'puffer'. However, more recently it has been recognised that spacers have other advantages as well. In fact, a combination of a puffer and a spacer is more efficient than a nebuliser pump in delivering medications deep into the lungs.

The advantages of using a puffer and a spacer are as follows.

- They deliver a more effective dose of medications to the lungs than either a puffer alone or a nebuliser pump.
- They are portable and easy to use; they don't need an electricity supply (as a pump does).
- Medications produce fewer side-effects with spacers than with pumps.
- They are inexpensive.
- They are easy to care for.

Caring for a spacer at home

Although it might seem strange, a sparkling clean spacer (such as one washed in a dishwasher) is *not* as efficient as a used spacer. This is because a sparkling clean spacer allows a build-up of static electricity on the inner surface, and this makes the spacer less efficient. A used spacer is a more efficient spacer.

A sparkling clean spacer is not as efficient as a used spacer.

Spacers should therefore be washed only about once a month—unless they are being used frequently for a few days (every four hours, or more often); if so, they should be washed once a week. If it is necessary to wash the spacer, it should be washed in warm soapy water (not disinfectants) and then allowed to drip dry. It should not be rinsed or wiped dry. The soapy solution forms a useful anti-static barrier on the inner surface.

Chapter 6

Vomiting and Diarrhoea

Framework of the chapter

The most common cause of vomiting and diarrhoea in children is *gastroenteritis*—which means inflammation of the stomach and intestines. In the vast majority of cases, a child with vomiting and diarrhoea will be suffering from some form of gastroenteritis. This chapter will therefore concentrate on gastroenteritis—but the chapter also discusses 'warning' signs and symptoms of *other* causes of vomiting and diarrhoea in children.

Framework of chapter

This chapter discusses vomiting and diarrhoea in children. The chapter covers the following subjects:

Causes of vomiting and diarrhoea

As previously noted, in the vast majority of cases a child with vomiting and diarrhoea will be suffering from some form of *gastroenteritis*. However, there are several other causes.

The causes of vomiting and diarrhoea can be summarised as follows:

- gastroenteritis of various sorts;
- infections in other parts of the body—such as urinary tract infection, pneumonia, or septicaemia ('blood poisoning');
- serious abdominal problems that require surgery (such as appendicitis); and
- other conditions (such as diabetes; or reactions to antibiotics and other medications).

Many of these conditions can be diagnosed only by health professionals, and many of the conditions listed here require special tests to make the diagnosis. If parents and carers are worried about a child with vomiting and diarrhoea, they should suspect that something other than gastroenteritis might be causing the problem. They should therefore seek medical attention.

In deciding whether to seek extra help for a child with vomiting and diarrhoea, parents and carers should be alert for certain signs and symptoms. They should *not* assume that the cause is 'only gastro' if:

- the child looks very sick, has a high temperature, and is 'toxic';
- the child has severe abdominal pain or tenderness of the abdomen;
- the child vomits blood or bile; or
- the child has prolonged vomiting *without* diarrhoea—because the diagnosis is very unlikely to be gastroenteritis if there is significant vomiting *but no diarrhoea*.

If any of the above signs and symptoms are present, the cause of the vomiting and diarrhoea is less likely to be gastroenteritis—and extra help should be sought. In particular, children with gastroenteritis do *not* usually have severe abdominal pain and are *not* usually very 'toxic'.

Seek medical help if ...

Warning signs and symptoms

Parents and carers should be aware of the following 'warning' signs and symptoms in a child with vomiting and diarrhoea. They should seek a medical opinion if:

- the child looks very sick, has a high temperature, and is 'toxic';
- the child has severe abdominal pain or tenderness of the abdomen;
- the child vomits blood or bile; or
- the child has prolonged vomiting *without* diarrhoea.

Other situations requiring a medical opinion

In addition to the 'warning' signs and symptoms listed above, parents and carers should seek a medical opinion if:

- the child is a neonate (within four weeks of birth); or
- the child has a *long-term* problem and is 'failing to thrive'.

In addition to the signs and symptoms listed above, parents and carers should seek medical assistance if the child is a neonate (within four weeks of birth). This is because these little babies require expert care—even if the problem is gastroenteritis.

Finally, the problem is unlikely to be gastroenteritis if the child has a *long-term* problem and is 'failing to thrive'.

Technical terms used in this chapter

This chapter uses some technical terms as a 'shorthand' way of describing what happens in gastroenteritis. Most of these are explained in the text, but this list might also be helpful.

Antibiotics
Medications that kill bacteria

Dehydration
Lack of normal level of fluid in the body

Gastroenteritis
Inflammation of the stomach and intestines—caused by various microbes

Incubation period
The time from when a child gets an infection until he or she becomes unwell

Microbe
Microscopic organisms that can cause disease (mainly bacteria or viruses)

Oral rehydration
Replacement of fluid by drinking through the mouth

Rehydration
Replacement of fluid to restore normal levels of fluid in the body

Secretory glands
Glands that put out fluid

Sign
Something that a parent or carer notices in a sick child (such as a rash)

Symptom
Something that the sick child complains about but other people cannot see (such as pain)

Signs and symptoms of gastroenteritis

The term 'gastroenteritis' means inflammation of the stomach and intestines. The inflammation nearly always causes diarrhoea, and often causes vomiting. It is one of the most common illnesses of childhood.

The most important signs and symptoms are, of course, diarrhoea and vomiting. This is usually of sudden onset with no preceding signs that the child is unwell. Diarrhoea is more common than vomiting; indeed, some cases of gastroenteritis have no vomiting at all. As previously noted, the diagnosis is very unlikely to be gastroenteritis if there is significant vomiting *but no diarrhoea.*

The diagnosis is very unlikely to be gastroenteritis if there is significant vomiting but no diarrhoea.

Other signs and symptoms that might be present include:

- poor appetite;
- fever; and
- abdominal cramps.

However, as previously noted, if a child is *very unwell* (especially with severe abdominal pain), the problem might be something other than gastroenteritis.

The main concern with gastroenteritis is possible *dehydration.* Depending on the degree of dehydration, gastroenteritis can vary from a mild illness that causes some inconvenience to a severe life-threatening illness.

Causes of gastroenteritis

There are many microbes that can cause gastroenteritis. These can include various sorts of viruses, bacteria, and parasites. The most common causes are:

- *viruses:* rotaviruses; adenoviruses;
- *bacteria: Campylobacter*; *Salmonella*; *Shigella*; *E. Coli*;
- *parasites: Giardia lamblia*; *Cryptospiridium*

Rotaviruses

Rotaviruses are easily the most common cause of gastroenteritis worldwide—especially in underdeveloped countries. In Western countries they cause about 50% of severe cases (those that are admitted to hospital).

Rotaviruses are easily the most common cause of gastroenteritis worldwide.

The virus is usually transmitted from hand to mouth, or by ingestion of contaminated food. The incubation period (from when the virus enters the body until signs and symptoms develop) is about 15–30 hours. The virus causes inflammation and damage to the mucosa (inner lining) of the intestine, and this causes diarrhoea.

The child usually develops a fever (about 38°C or above) for approximately 48 hours. This is usually accompanied by nausea and vomiting, followed by frequent, watery diarrhoea. The diarrhoea can last for more than a week.

Salmonella

Salmonella bacteria are carried by infected poultry (including eggs), pets, and animals. The bacteria are spread by hand-to-mouth transmission or by ingestion of contaminated food.

The incubation period is 6–72 hours, and the bacteria penetrate into the small bowel wall causing inflammation and extensive destruction.

The illness is characterised by rapid onset, nausea and vomiting, abdominal pain (often quite severe), and diarrhoea with blood and mucus.

Shigella

Shigella bacteria are transmitted directly from person to person, or indirectly via cutlery and crockery.

The incubation period is usually 2–4 days, but can be as long as seven days. The bacteria produce a toxin (poison) that causes superficial ulceration of the bowel wall and stimulates the loss of fluid from the bowel.

The illness can be variable, but it usually produces a sudden high temperature (40°C), followed by cramping abdominal pain and diarrhoea (often with blood and mucus).

Giardia

Giardia lamblia is a parasite that lives in the small bowel of certain people. It can also grow in water tanks (usually if stagnant). It is mainly spread by person-to-person contact, although it can be spread from infected water supplies or animals. The parasite lives in the duodenum (upper part of the small intestine) where it causes inflammation.

The diarrhoea of *Giardia* is typically "bulky" and foul-smelling.

The incubation period is variable, but it usually takes 1–3 weeks to have an effect. People with a *Giardia* infection usually feel unwell in the upper abdomen (perhaps with vague pain in the same area). They then develop cramping abdominal pains and diarrhoea. The diarrhoea is typically 'bulky' and foul-smelling. If the problem goes on for some time, children can develop signs and symptoms of malnutrition.

Dehydration

Children more at risk

Children become dehydrated more quickly than adults. There are several reasons for this. The first is concerned with the relative size of the small intestine, and the second is concerned with the way in which the kidneys work.

- Compared to overall size, the small intestine of a child is significantly longer than that of an adult. The length of a child's small intestine is about six times the child's body length, whereas the length of an adult's small intestine is only about four times the adult's body length. But the pattern of secretory glands (that is, glands that put out fluid) in the two intestines is the same. So if the small intestine is inflamed (as a result of gastroenteritis), a child will lose significantly more fluid than the adult (as a proportion of body size).
- The kidneys of a child (especially an infant) are less mature than those of an adult and are less able to retain fluid.

Children become dehydrated more quickly than adults.

Assessing dehydration

In assessing the severity of dehydration, medical and nursing textbooks often talk about the *percentage of weight* that the child has lost as a result of losing too much fluid. The books then talk about the severity of dehydration in terms of an exact percentage of weight loss—for example, 'mild dehydration' is said to be equivalent to 3–5% dehydration. But this is very difficult to judge at the time. In fact, even doctors and nurses tend to measure precise percentages *after* the event—when the child is well again!

Because it is so difficult to *measure* the degree of dehydration precisely, it is more useful if parents and carers make a sensible judgment of the child's *overall state of health*. They should observe the child's general behaviour, general appearance, and urine output. The following notes will help in making these sorts of sensible assessments.

Mild dehydration

A child with mild dehydration is not very sick at all. The child might be thirsty and restless, but the child is otherwise (in general) quite well.

A child with this degree of dehydration will get better with oral fluids as the gastroenteritis settles down. No medical care is required at this stage.

Moderate dehydration

A child with moderate dehydration is obviously unwell. The child is thirsty and has decreased urine output. The child is usually lethargic, but might be restless and irritable if touched—for example, the child might be lying quietly in a cot, but resists being touched or handled.

The child usually has sunken eyes and a sunken abdomen. A healthy small child normally has a 'pot belly' (even when lying down), but a child with moderate dehydration has a flat or sunken abdomen.

The child often has a dry tongue and mouth. There might be an absence of tears from the eyes when crying.

The child will have a rapid pulse and might have signs of poor circulation—such as a mottled appearance to the lower legs and feet.

An important sign in assessing moderate and severe dehydration is known as 'capillary refill'. This is described in the Box below. In performing the 'capillary refill' test, pale skin should become pink again within two seconds. If it takes longer, the child is likely to be moderately or severely dehydrated.

In performing the "capillary refill" test, pale skin should become pink again within two seconds.

A moderate degree of dehydration requires medical assessment and treatment.

Capillary refill

An important test for moderate or severe dehydration is the test known as 'capillary refill'. This is easy to do and gives a good indication of significant dehydration.

Step 1

The parent lies the child down and exposes the child's chest.

Step 2

Using a fingertip, the parent presses firmly on the skin overlying the sternum (breast bone). Firm pressure is maintained for five seconds.

Step 3

Remove the pressure and observe the child's skin. The area where pressure has been applied will be white.

Step 4

Watch to see how long the skin takes to become pink again. *The skin should return to a pink colour within two seconds.*

Severe dehydration

A child with severe dehydration is very unwell. The child is very thirsty and has no urine output. He or she is cold and clammy to touch, and the limbs are often bluish in colour.

Infants are weak and 'limp'; they are often drowsy and can even be comatose. Older children are apprehensive, weak, and lethargic.

Both infants and children have a rapid, feeble pulse. They have sunken eyes and very dry tongue and mouth.

A severe degree of dehydration requires urgent medical treatment.

A severe degree of dehydration requires urgent medical treatment.

Management of gastroenteritis

Oral rehydration

In the vast majority of cases of mild–moderate dehydration, it is possible (and desirable) to rehydrate children at home using oral fluids. In most cases, this can be done using the child's usual preferred fluids. For example, a breast-fed infant should continue to receive breast-feeding, and a formula-fed infant should continue to receive his or her normal formula. If extra fluids are required for rehydration, the best fluids are more breast-feeding or extra water between formula feeds. Lactose-free formulas are rarely required for infants and young children with gastroenteritis, but they might be recommended if the diarrhoea lasts more than 10–14 days.

In the vast majority of cases, it is possible (and desirable) to rehydrate children at home using oral fluids.

In children who have more severe gastroenteritis, other fluids might be recommended. These can include:

- dilute fruit juice (about a quarter of normal strength);
- dilute lemonade (about a quarter of normal strength);
- dilute cordial (about a quarter of normal strength);
- sugar solution (about one teaspoon of sugar in 240 millilitres of water); or
- 'Gastrolyte', 'Pedialyte', or 'Repalyte' solutions (specially prepared solutions of fluid and electrolytes—vital chemicals that are lost with vomiting and diarrhoea).

These fluids are best given in small volumes often—for example, it is better to give 10 millilitres every 5–10 minutes, rather than 100 millilitres every hour. If making any of these solutions up from a powder or tablet (especially 'Gastrolyte' or similar), parents should follow the manufacturer's instructions carefully and never add cordial or sugar to improve the taste.

Fluids are best given in small volumes often.

Icy poles are a good way of getting children to suck fluid slowly. 'Hydralyte' icy poles are especially good in this regard—because they supply the same sorts of electrolytes (vital chemicals) that are provided in 'Gastrolyte'.

Food

In the past, parents used to be advised to stop children eating for several days in succession—or even until the diarrhoea ceases. However, there is no evidence that avoiding food makes much difference to the child's rate of recovery—in most cases the diarrhoea will continue for 7–10 days anyway.

The best advice is to observe the child and see how he or she feels. The child will probably not feel like eating for a day or two. When the child does feel like eating, he or she should be allowed to do so. Suitable foods include:

- rice;
- wheat products (bread and cereals);
- grated raw apple (left to go brown);
- mashed banana; and
- yoghurt.

In general, the child should be allowed to eat whatever he or she wants. The child should be back on a full normal diet and fluids within 48–72 hours, even if the diarrhoea continues. And, as noted previously, parents and carers should be aware that the diarrhoea will probably go on for 7–10 days anyway.

Medications

In general, anti-vomiting and anti-diarrhoeal medications should be avoided in children. The potential side-effects are more of a problem than the symptoms.

Prevention of spread

Gastroenteritis is caused by the ingestion of microbes (viruses, bacteria, or parasites) from other people or from infected food. These microbes can be spread from person to person by direct contact, or by indirect contact (via cutlery and crockery).

To avoid spreading gastroenteritis, the most important precaution is thorough handwashing. People should wash their hands thoroughly:

- after attending to a child with gastroenteritis;
- after changing nappies;
- before preparing food; and
- after visiting the toilet.

Parents and carers should also ensure that children wash their hands properly.

Children with vomiting and diarrhoea should be kept away from other children while they are unwell. Sick children should not return to child care or school until at least 24 hours after the last episode of vomiting or diarrhoea.

Correct techniques should *always* be strictly followed for storing and preparing food.

The microbes that cause gastroenteritis can also be spread by poor food handling. Correct techniques should *always* be strictly followed for storing and preparing food.

Chapter 7

Abdominal Pain

Causes of significant abdominal pain

Abdominal pain is a common problem in children of all ages. There are many possible causes—in fact, there are too many to list in a book such as this on basic care of sick children. Many of these problems go away without any specific medical attention. Parents and carers are therefore most interested in knowing about the *more serious* causes of abdominal pain—such as appendicitis and other problems that might require medical assessment and, possibly, surgery.

Framework of chapter

This chapter discusses the more common and more serious causes of abdominal pain in children. The chapter covers the following subjects:

Making an assessment

Faced with a child who is complaining of abdominal pain, parents and carers need to sort out more serious problems from ones that don't really matter. Even if they can't make a definite diagnosis themselves, parents and carers can get a clearer idea of the nature and severity of the problem by asking themselves the following sorts of questions:

- When was the child last completely well? Is this pain something that has come on quite suddenly 'out of the blue', or has the pain been 'niggling' for a few days? When *exactly* did the pain start?
- What was the first thing that went wrong? Was the pain the first symptom, or has the child had other signs and symptoms (such as lack of appetite, runny nose, cough, and so on)?
- If the child has vomiting and/or diarrhoea, what came first—the pain or the vomiting/diarrhoea?
- Where exactly is the pain? In some cases it is impossible for a child (or an adult!) to be specific about the *exact* location of the pain. However, it is still worth asking a child whether he or she can show you where the pain is.
- How severe is the pain? Older children can be asked to 'grade' their pain on a scale of 1–10. But younger children do not have enough experience of earlier pains to make a meaningful assessment. However, whatever the age of the child, it is still worth asking how bad the pain feels.
- How is the child behaving as a result of the pain? Is the child lying still or rolling around? Can the child walk? Can the child sleep despite the pain? Was the child actually woken up by the pain?

By asking these sorts of questions, parents and carers get a clearer idea of the whole picture—rather than a vague impression of a distressed child with a worrying problem. Although they are not expected to make a definite diagnosis on their own, parents and carers can make a reasonable assessment of the severity of the problem. In addition, the answers to these questions will gather valuable information that might be useful for doctors and nurses later on.

Appendicitis

What is appendicitis?

Appendicitis is inflammation of the appendix. The appendix is a small 'finger-like' projection from the intestine, situated in the bottom right-hand corner of the abdomen. The appendix contains a large number of white blood cells and is therefore very prone to inflammation if it becomes blocked or infected.

Appendicitis is most common in school-age children, adolescents, and young adults.

Appendicitis can occur at any age—from the very young to very old. However, it is most common in school-age children (usually older than six years), adolescents, and young adults.

(It should be noted that a very small proportion of people have their appendix on the *left* side of the body—rather than the right. But this is rare, and when it does occur it often runs in families, and is frequently known by members of those families. In making comments about appendicitis, this chapter assumes that the child's appendix is on the *right* side of the abdomen—which covers the overwhelming majority of children with appendicitis.)

Technical terms used in this chapter

This chapter uses some technical terms as a 'shorthand' way of describing what happens in abdominal pain. Most of these are explained in the text, but this list might also be helpful.

Analgesics
Pain-killers

Antibiotics
Medications that kill bacteria

Appendicitis
Inflammation of the appendix

Gastroenteritis
Inflammation of the stomach and intestines—caused by various microbes

Intussusception
A condition in which one portion of the intestine is *telescoped inside* the next portion of bowel; (pronounced 'in-ta-sus-SEP-sh'-n')

Lymph nodes
Collections of white blood cells for fighting infection; nodes occur in various parts of the body (including around the throat, in the groins, and in the abdomen); often mistakenly called 'glands'

Microbe
Microscopic organisms that can cause disease (mainly bacteria or viruses)

Recurrent
Something that comes back again

Sign
Something that a parent or carer notices in a sick child (such as a rash)

Symptom
Something that the sick child complains about but other people cannot see (such as pain)

Urinary tract infections
An infection of the urinary tract—especially the bladder and/or kidneys; often called a 'UTI'

Signs and symptoms

The 'classic' signs and symptoms of appendicitis are not always present, but most cases of appendicitis start with a day or two of the child feeling unwell, with loss of appetite and nausea. Some children also vomit—although this is not a major problem in appendicitis. Some diarrhoea is occasionally present.

The child often has a mild temperature (usually about 37.5°C). It is unusual for the temperature to be higher than 38°C in school-age children or older. In younger children the temperature can be higher, and the illness usually progresses more quickly in every respect.

The pain usually begins around the umbilicus ('belly button'). It is often vague and difficult to 'pinpoint' at this stage. The pain later becomes more severe and easier to locate as it moves down to the area over the appendix—in the bottom right-hand corner of the abdomen (closer to the groin than the umbilicus). The child can usually locate the pain in this area. If parents apply gentle hand pressure in this area, they will find that the child is very tender. In most cases the child's abdominal muscles will tense up and resist any pressure being applied. However, parents should not apply pressure to the abdomen if the child is in a great deal of pain and obviously very sick.

The pain usually begins around the umbilicus … but later becomes more severe and easier to locate as it moves down to the area over the appendix.

If the child is not too sick, parents and carers can carry out the 'hop test'. This is described in the Box below. If the child is willing to hop on his or her right leg, the diagnosis is *unlikely* to be appendicitis.

The 'hop test' for appendicitis

If a child with abdominal pain is not very unwell, parents and carers can carry out the 'hop test' to check for appendicitis.

Step 1

Ask the child to stand in a clear space (away from furniture) with legs together.

Step 2

Ask the child to lift the right foot from the ground and hop on the left leg. (This is a 'practice' hop.)

Step 3

Ask the child to put both feet on the ground again.

Step 4

Now ask the child to lift the left foot from the ground and hop on the *right* leg. (This is the 'real' test.)

Assessment of 'hop test'

A child with appendicitis will be reluctant to do Step 4. The child might refuse. Some children might try to hop on the right leg but then experience significant pain in doing so. A child who is able to hop on the right leg is unlikely to have appendicitis.

Management

If appendicitis is suspected, the child needs to be taken to a doctor or hospital for assessment. If the diagnosis is confirmed, surgery is likely to be required.

Constipation

What is constipation?

Constipation is the most common cause of abdominal pain in children over two years of age. It should always be considered when a child complains of abdominal pain.

In deciding whether a child has constipation, parents and carers should not be as concerned about the *frequency* of bowel actions as the *nature* of the bowel actions. Some children do not have a bowel action for several days. Then, when they *do* have a bowel action, they have no problem. So constipation is not defined by how many days a child goes without having a bowel action; rather, constipation is defined as having *hard stools that are difficult to pass*.

Signs and symptoms of constipation

Constipation can cause quite severe abdominal pain. Children with constipation also often have loss of appetite and irritability. Vomiting on its own (with no other signs and symptoms) is not likely to be due to constipation.

Causes of constipation

Some children are born with a reduced number of nerves in the wall of their large intestine. This is known as 'neuronal intestinal dysplasia' (NID). Children with NID have decreased movement of their intestine, and this causes chronic constipation. These cases usually become apparent in infancy or very early childhood. They are difficult to treat and require specialist assessment and management.

Apart from NID, other physical causes of constipation include:

- poor diet;
- inadequate fluid intake;
- reduced activity; and
- painful conditions of the anus (such as tears or fissures).

Psychological and social causes can include:

- uncooperative toddler behaviour—in which a toddler wishes to assert his or her independence by refusing to cooperate with parents in their attempts to teach toilet training; and
- sexual abuse—in which psychological trauma and physical injury can combine to cause constipation.

Management

The management of constipation can be divided into: (i) treatment of the immediate problem; and (ii) long-term management of the constipation.

Immediate treatment

If the constipation is causing significant pain, the child will probably require assessment and treatment by a doctor or hospital. The child might require analgesics (pain killers) and an enema to clear the constipation.

Any child with constipation who is under three months of age should be referred for specialist assessment—in case the child has a physical problem with the bowel.

Any child with constipation who is under three months of age should be referred for specialist assessment.

Long-term management

The most important aspects of long-term management are proper diet and adequate fluids. Parents and carers should ensure that the child drinks clear fluids (water, fruit juice, cordial) regularly and frequently. The child's diet should include high-fibre foods—such as cereals and fresh fruit.

Regular toileting habits can be useful in some cases—especially for impatient and busy children who are 'too busy' to sit on the toilet for any length of time. They should be encouraged to sit on the toilet—for a leisurely period of time—at certain agreed times each day.

Laxatives might be required in some cases. There is a large range of laxatives available, and parents might require advice from a doctor, nurse, or pharmacist in making the right decision. In general, it is best to use the 'bulk-forming' laxatives (such as prune juice, 'Metamucil' or 'Senokot') as first choice, rather than the 'lubricant' laxatives (such as 'Coloxyl'). Laxatives should not be used on a long-term basis without medical advice.

Intussusception

What is intussusception?

The word 'intussusception' (pronounced 'in-ta-sus-SEP-sh'-n') means 'to receive within'. It is used to describe a condition in which one portion of the intestine (usually the small intestine) is *telescoped inside* the next portion of bowel (usually the large intestine). It causes severe abdominal pain, and it can be a serious condition requiring surgery.

Causes of intussusception

In most cases, there is no obvious cause. In some cases, the child is born with an abnormality of the bowel wall. In other cases, the problem appears to follow inflammation of the lymph nodes around the bowel; in these cases the problem often follows the child having a viral upper respiratory tract infection (which also affects the lymph nodes of the abdomen).

It tends to occur in younger children (aged three months to five years). About 50% of cases occur in infants aged 3–12 months. Boys are three times as likely as girls to have intussusception.

Signs and symptoms

The diagnosis of intussusception is usually made by observing the child. The pattern of signs and symptoms is usually typical and diagnostic of intussusception.

The condition usually affects infants. The baby is *very* distressed indeed—but only in 'spasms'. The baby cries loudly and screams with pain for a few minutes. He or she is usually red-faced and obviously *very* distressed. Children with intussusception typically pull their knees up to the abdomen during a spasm. They then relax, and although they might be pale and lethargic, they appear to be relatively 'normal' for a variable time (a few minutes to half an hour). Then there is another severe spasm of pain, screaming, and crying.

The pattern of signs and symptoms is usually typical and diagnostic of intussusception.

Parents and carers will usually recognise that these episodes of crying and screaming are quite different from anything that they have observed in the child before. The pattern of crying is quite different from an 'irritable cry', or a 'hungry cry', or other forms of distress. The baby is obviously experiencing severe and overwhelming spasms of pain.

In the later stages of the illness, the child might pass a bowel action that contains blood and mucus. This looks very much like 'red-currant jelly'—and such a typical 'red-currant jelly stool' is diagnostic of intussusception. However, this is a late sign, and it indicates that the bowel has already suffered significant damage. It is desirable that all cases are detected and treated before they reach this advanced stage.

Treatment

Intussusception is a potentially serious disease. If it goes on without treatment, it can cause severe bowel damage and death can occur. Intussusception therefore obviously requires urgent medical assessment and treatment—usually in a hospital.

Parents and carers who are faced with a baby who is screaming in agony are likely to seek such assistance. If they see the pattern of signs and symptoms described previously (spasms of *severe* pain and crying), parents and carers can often make the diagnosis themselves and seek appropriate medical assistance promptly.

Intussusception is a potentially serious disease; if it goes on without treatment, it can cause severe bowel damage and death.

Once the child reaches hospital, treatment varies. In most cases, especially those detected early, the intussusception can be relieved without surgery—by using a special sort of enema. However, parents and carers should be aware that the problem can come back. In these cases, surgery is usually required.

Urinary tract infections

What is a urinary tract infection?

A urinary tract infection (often referred to as a 'UTI') is a bacterial infection of the urinary tract—especially the bladder and/or the kidneys. The bacteria usually get into the urinary tract 'from below', and later infect the bladder and kidneys.

There is a wide variety of bacteria that can cause UTIs, and virtually all of them can be successfully treated with a course of antibiotics. In a minority of cases the problem is recurrent (that is, it comes back again). This can cause long-term damage to the kidneys. Therefore, all children who have a UTI should be seen by a doctor. Appropriate investigations should be undertaken to ensure that no kidney damage occurs.

All children who have a UTI should be seen by a doctor.

Signs and symptoms

Although UTIs can produce abdominal pain, many cases do not have abdominal pain as a first symptom. These cases first develop vague 'non-specific' signs and symptoms—such as fever, irritability, poor feeding, and vomiting. Only later do they develop abdominal pain.

The abdominal pain can be in the lower abdomen (over the bladder) or in the loins (over the kidneys). The pain can be a vague ache, or it can be quite severe and disabling. If pain is felt in the loins (over the kidneys), children will usually be tender (sore to touch) in that area.

In most cases, UTIs also cause painful urination. This is often described as 'burning' or 'stinging'. It is also common to have increased frequency of urination—often with only small amounts of urine being passed each time.

In older children, this combination of signs and symptoms will usually enable parents and carers to make the right diagnosis. However, in babies and small children (those still using nappies), it is often difficult for parents and carers to make a clear link between the child's illness and the passing of urine. In these cases the diagnosis can be more difficult to make.

Treatment

If a UTI is suspected, medical assistance should be obtained. Doctors and nurses will collect urine and perform tests to confirm the diagnosis. Antibiotics will be prescribed to kill the bacteria that are responsible for the infection. Suitable investigations will then be undertaken.

Parents and carers should never ignore a UTI in a child; every case needs to be properly treated and investigated.

Parents and carers should never ignore a UTI in a child. Every case needs to be properly treated and investigated.

Other causes of abdominal pain

There are many other causes of abdominal pain. As previously noted, it is simply not possible to discuss them all in a book on basic care. However, the more common and important conditions have been discussed here. In addition to the problems already discussed in this chapter, parents and carers should be aware that, among other things, abdominal pain can also be due to:

- bowel obstruction—usually marked by severe vomiting and a lack of bowel actions;
- gastroenteritis—see Chapter 6, 'Vomiting and Diarrhoea', page 65; and
- 'strangulated' hernias—usually associated with severe localised pain, and (possibly) a swelling in the groin or scrotum.

In adolescent girls, the possibility of ectopic pregnancy and gynaecological infections should also be kept in mind. Although parents and carers might be reluctant to consider this possibility in younger teenagers, they should remember that these conditions can be serious (or even life-threatening) and it might be necessary to discuss these possibilities to avoid serious consequences.

Chapter 8

Headaches

A common problem

Headaches are common among children. Approximately 40% of children have a significant headache by the age of 7 years, and approximately 75% have one by the age of 15 years.

Most headaches are not serious. However, some are caused by a significant medical problem, and a small proportion are due to life-threatening conditions.

Types of headaches

Because headaches are so common, it is not surprising that there are many possible causes. For convenience, headaches can be divided into two groups:

- acute headaches; and
- recurrent headaches.

Framework of chapter

This chapter discusses headaches under the following headings:

Acute headaches

When doctors and nurses use the word 'acute', they do not necessarily mean 'serious'. The word 'acute' is used to describe the *timeframe* of an illness (not its severity). For example, an 'acute' pain is a pain that has started only recently (perhaps in the last few hours), whereas a 'chronic' pain is pain that has been present for a relatively long time (perhaps weeks).

An 'acute' headache is therefore a 'new' headache that has started only recently. Some of the more important causes of acute headaches are listed in the Box below. Most of these are discussed later in this chapter.

Causes of acute headaches in children

An 'acute headache' is a 'new' headache that has started only recently. Some of the more important causes of acute headaches are:

- generalised illnesses (infections, fevers, and so on);
- conditions affecting the face (sinusitis, tooth infections, ear infections, and so on);
- head injuries;
- meningitis and encephalitis (inflammation of the coverings of the spinal cord and brain); and
- internal bleeding (subarachnoid haemorrhage).

Recurrent headaches

The term 'recurrent' refers to conditions that keep coming back. A 'recurrent headache' is thus a repeated headache that keeps coming back over a period of time.

Some of the more important causes of recurrent headaches are listed in the Box below. Most of these are discussed later in this chapter.

Causes of recurrent headaches in children

A 'recurrent headache' is a repeated headache that keeps coming back over a period of time. Some of the more important causes of recurrent headaches are:

- migraine headaches;
- tension headaches;
- raised intra-cranial pressure—conditions that cause increased pressure inside the skull (brain tumours and so on); and
- behavioural problems.

Patterns of headaches

It is not easy for parents and carers to diagnose the many possible causes of headaches. In many cases (especially with recurrent headaches) a proper medical assessment and special tests are needed before a diagnosis can be made.

Parents and carers can assist doctors and nurses by taking careful note of the overall pattern of the child's headaches. The diagram in Figure 8.1 (below) is useful in this regard.

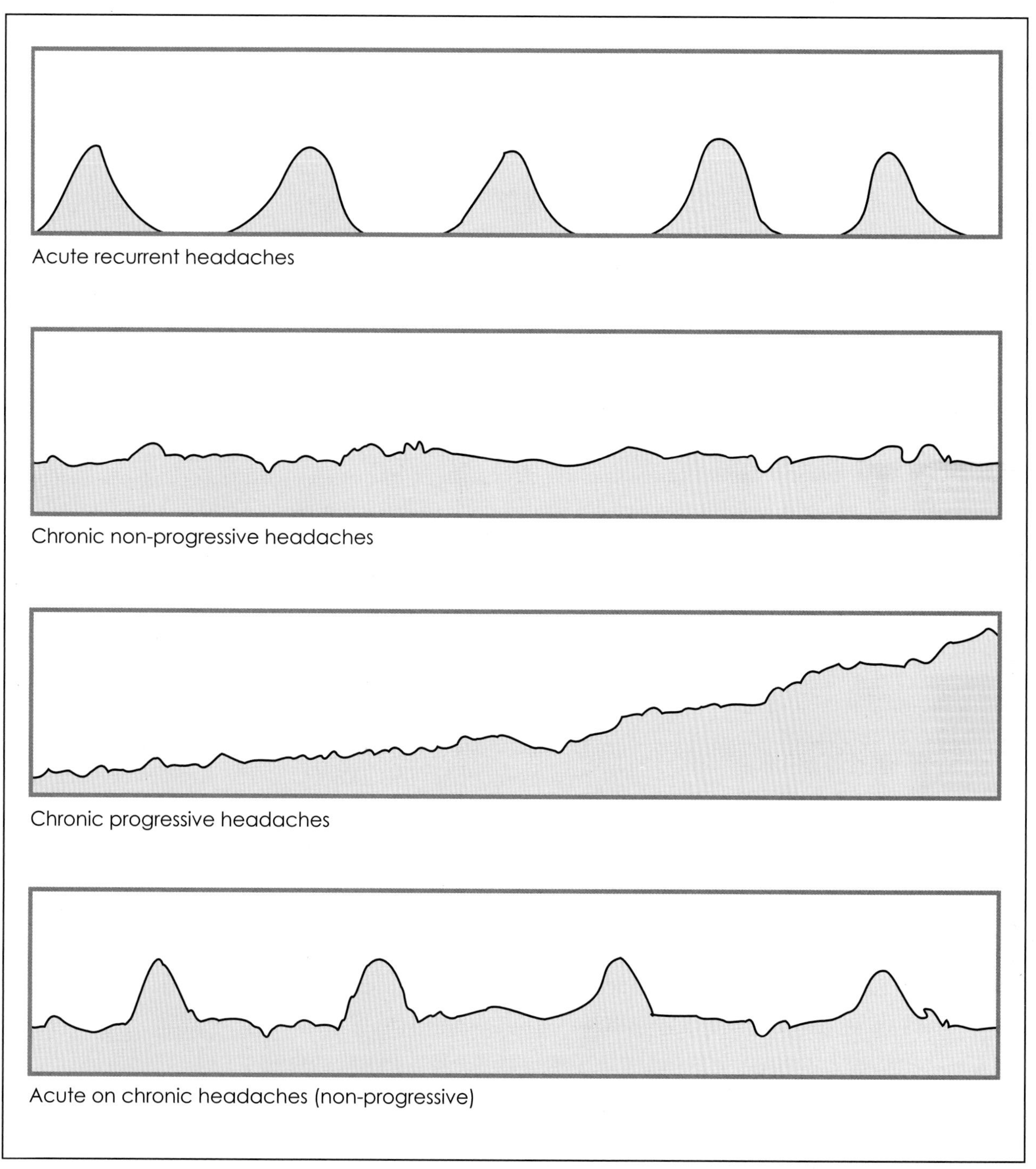

Figure 8.1 Patterns of headaches
AUTHOR'S PRESENTATION, ADAPTED FROM AN ORIGINAL DIAGRAM PREPARED BY THE ROYAL CHILDREN'S HOSPITAL, MELBOURNE

Figure 8.1 shows various patterns of headaches. These can be summarised as follows.

- The first pattern shows 'acute recurrent headaches'—these are short-lived headaches that keep coming back.
- The second pattern shows 'chronic non-progressive headaches'—low-grade chronic headaches, present most of the time, but not getting any worse.

- The third pattern shows 'chronic progressive headaches'—chronic headaches, present most of the time, and getting worse.
- The fourth pattern shows 'acute on chronic headaches, non-progressive'—low-grade chronic headaches, present most of the time, with intermittent flare-ups, but not getting any worse.

If parents and carers are able to describe a general pattern of headaches along these lines, it will be easier for doctors and nurses to make the correct diagnosis from among the hundreds of possible causes of headaches.

Common and important causes of headaches

Because headaches are so common, and because there is such a wide variety of causes, it is not possible for a 'Basic Guide' book such as this to give a full account of *every* possible cause. However, the following causes of headaches are worthy of note because they are common or important.

Generalised illnesses

Many common illnesses can be associated with headaches. For example, a child with a viral illness and a fever will often complain of a headache. This is especially likely to happen if an upper respiratory tract infection has become more generalised—such as when the 'flu' produces aches and pains all over the body (including a headache). In some cases, the generalised illness that is causing the headache might be a more serious condition—such as pneumonia (lung infection) or septicaemia (blood poisoning).

If a headache is severe and persistent, parents and carers should take the child to see a doctor.

A headache that is due to a generalised illness does not necessarily mean that the illness is serious. However, if a headache is *severe* and *persistent*, parents and carers should take the child to see a doctor.

Conditions affecting the face

Many localised conditions that affect the face and ears can cause headaches (or what children sometimes call 'headaches'). These common conditions can include:

- sinusitis (inflammation of the sinuses in the cheek bones and forehead);
- dental caries (tooth and gum infections); and
- otitis media (middle ear infections).

Another condition that is less well known is 'TMJ syndrome'—which can occur in children, adolescents, and adults. 'TMJ syndrome' is due to soreness in the joint where the lower jaw is attached to the skull (just in front of the ear). This joint is known as the 'tempero-mandibular joint' or 'TMJ'. When this joint becomes sore (which is called 'TMJ syndrome') pain is caused by simply opening and closing the jaw. The child can experience shooting pains in the joint itself, in the jaw, or up into the head.

If a headache is caused by one of these localised conditions affecting the face, it is usually possible for parents and carers to work out what is going on—because the pain is more-or-less localised to the affected area (or it is likely to be more severe in these areas). However, this is

Technical terms used in this chapter

This chapter uses some technical terms as a 'shorthand' way of describing what happens with headaches. Most of these are explained in the text, but this list might also be helpful.

Acute
Something that has started only recently (perhaps in the last few hours)

Analgesics
Pain-killers

Chronic
Something that has been present for a relatively long time (perhaps weeks)

Photophobia
Dislike of the light

Recurrent
Something that comes back again

Sign
Something that a parent or carer notices in a sick child (such as a rash)

Symptom
Something that the sick child complains about but other people cannot see (such as pain)

Upper respiratory tract infections
Infections in the nose, throat, and upper airways (top part of the lungs)

not always easy in children because they sometimes have difficulty in knowing (or explaining) exactly where the pain is. In addition, some of these conditions can cause pain that spreads beyond the local area. For example, sinusitis often causes a 'spreading pain' that takes the pain beyond the sinuses themselves. Parents and carers should attempt to work out where the pain is coming from by asking the child about the pain and, if necessary, by gently examining the face, jaws, and ears.

Children sometimes have difficulty in knowing (or explaining) exactly where the pain is.

Head injury

Injuries to the head, both minor and major, can obviously cause headaches. If a child has suffered a head injury and has a headache that is persistent or severe, medical attention should be sought. For more on head injuries, see Chapter 11, 'Head Injuries', page 107.

Meningitis

Meningitis is inflammation of the membrane (covering) around the brain and spinal cord. It is usually caused by an infection.

Common and important causes of headaches

This portion of the chapter discusses some common and important causes of headaches under the following headings:

- Generalised illnesses (page 84)
- Conditions affecting the face (page 84)
- Head injury (page 85)
- Meningitis (page 85)
- Subarachnoid haemorrhage (page 86)
- Migraine headaches (page 87)
- Raised intra-cranial pressure (page 87)
- Tension headaches (page 88)

The signs and symptoms of meningitis can include headache, fever, stiff neck, and photophobia (dislike of the light). In more severe cases, the child might have vomiting and altered consciousness (such as drowsiness and confusion).

If parents and carers suspect that a child has meningitis, medical attention should immediately be sought.

Subarachnoid haemorrhage

The term 'subarachnoid' means 'under the arachnoid'. The brain is covered by three membranes, and the middle one of these is called the 'arachnoid'. A 'subarachnoid haemorrhage' is therefore a sudden leaking (haemorrhage) of blood from a blood vessel that is 'under the arachnoid' on the surface of the brain.

Subarachnoid haemorrhage can affect children and adults of all ages, but is most common in adults. Only a small proportion of cases occur in people younger than 20 years. However, parents and carers should be aware that subarachnoid haemorrhages can occur in adolescents and children.

The most common symptom of a subarachnoid haemorrhage is severe headache (usually at the back of the head), followed by neck stiffness, nausea, and vomiting.

The most common symptom of a subarachnoid haemorrhage is severe headache (usually at the back of the head), followed by neck stiffness, nausea, and vomiting. In severe cases, the person loses consciousness, and some have a seizure ('fit').

In most cases, a subarachnoid haemorrhage is due to the sudden leaking of blood from a weakness in the wall of one of the arteries to the brain. In most cases the artery has a balloon-like swelling, which is called an 'aneurysm'. This can begin to leak for no apparent reason. Other causes include high blood pressure, physical exertion, emotional stress, or head injury.

A subarachnoid haemorrhage can be very serious if not diagnosed and treated promptly. The haemorrhage can be fatal, or the person can be left with 'stroke-like' signs and symptoms. It is very important that urgent medical help is sought if a subarachnoid haemorrhage is suspected.

Migraine headaches

Migraine headaches *do* occur in children—commonly in a child with a family history of migraine or motion sickness (such as 'car sickness'). Migraine can be diagnosed in children as young as four years. By early high school, most boys 'outgrow' the condition; however, in girls it can persist (or even become worse)—probably because of hormonal factors.

Migraine occurs as a result of blood vessels in the brain constricting (narrowing) and then dilating (opening up). During the constriction phase, the child can have an 'aura'—an awareness that the headache is about to start. This can simply be a feeling that something is 'going wrong', or it can include changes in balance or vision (such as 'tunnel vision'). The blood vessels then dilate (open up) causing a headache.

Signs and symptoms of migraine include:

- headache;
- loss of appetite;
- nausea and vomiting;
- pallor (paleness);
- fatigue; and
- abdominal pain.

The headache is variable. It can be mild or severe, and it can be dull or throbbing. It might be localised to one side of the head or it can occur over all of the head. Most migraine headaches last 6–12 hours, but some can persist for several days.

Sometimes a pattern of 'trigger factors' can be noted. Trigger factors can include stress, exposure to tobacco smoke, missing meals, flashing lights, some medications, or certain foods (although this is more common in adults).

The diagnosis is made on the basis of the child's history—often looking back over a period of time. There is no single test that can definitely tell if a person has migraine. In a child, the diagnosis cannot usually be made before about the age of four years—because the child is unable to provide an accurate description of the symptoms before this. However, if a child is diagnosed with migraine at the age of 4–5 years, parents will often remark that the child has actually been 'like this' for several years (perhaps since the age of two years, or even younger).

The diagnosis is made on the basis of the child's history ... There is no single test that can definitely tell if a person has migraine.

There is no cure for migraine. Attempts should be made to avoid trigger factors. If a migraine occurs, the best treatment is rest in a quiet, darkened room. Simple painkillers (such as paracetamol or ibuprofen) should be given. Stronger painkillers (such as codeine) and anti-vomiting medication might be prescribed under medical supervision.

Raised intra-cranial pressure

There are various medical problems that can cause raised intra-cranial pressure (that is, increased pressure inside the skull). Brain tumours, abscesses, and so on can cause this problem.

These sorts of problems often (but not always) follow a typical pattern. This pattern consists of the child complaining of headache when he or she first wakes up in the morning. This headache might be associated with vomiting. Then the child begins to feel better. Often the child is quite well by mid-morning. The pattern is then repeated (more or less in the same way) in subsequent days and weeks. The headache is often made worse by coughing, sneezing, or bending. Over a period of time the headaches and vomiting become worse. The child might also develop other signs and symptoms.

This unusual pattern of illness can cause parents and carers to think that the child is trying to avoid school.

In many cases, this unusual pattern of illness (worse in the morning and better later in the day) can cause parents and carers to think that the child is trying to avoid school or pre-school. However, the pattern is typical of *raised intra-cranial pressure*, and parents and carers who note this sort of pattern should have the child assessed by a doctor.

Tension headaches

Tension headaches *do* occur in children—although less frequently than in adults. They can occur frequently (perhaps daily), or they can occur in 'episodes' (that is, every few weeks or so). The headache often affects the muscles at the back of the neck, and is more likely to occur at the end of the day (or after school).

It is difficult to be precise about management because each child's history and circumstances will be different. However, it is important to have a proper medical assessment to rule out more serious causes. It should never be assumed that a child's headaches are due to 'behavioural problems' or 'stress' unless other causes have been ruled out by thorough assessment and examination.

Chapter 9

Dermatitis

What is dermatitis?

'Dermatitis' is a general term which means, literally, 'inflammation of the skin'. There are many causes and types of dermatitis. In some cases the inflammation is caused by direct irritation from various things in the external environment—chemicals, infections, insect bites, and so on. In other cases the inflammation is caused by allergic reactions. In many cases the exact cause is unknown or never identified. In some cases, mild inflammation is made worse by a child scratching at an itchy bite or rash.

This chapter discusses some of the more common causes of dermatitis in children—including eczema, psoriasis, fungal infections, scabies, and head lice.

Dermatitis means, literally, "inflammation of the skin".

Framework of chapter

This chapter discusses some of the more common causes of dermatitis in children under the following headings:

Eczema

A common condition

Eczema is a common inflammatory condition of the skin. The name comes from the Greek word for 'boil over' or 'break out'. About 20% of children (1 in 5) have eczema of some degree. The exact cause of eczema is unknown, but it appears to be a hypersensitivity reaction (an 'over-reaction') of the skin to the environment. It is often called 'atopic dermatitis'—which means that the child has an inherited tendency to allergic reactions (such as hayfever, asthma, and eczema).

Signs and symptoms

Eczema is a red, itchy area of dermatitis affecting one or more parts of the body. It can occur anywhere—including the face, limbs, and trunk. The rash is associated with intense itching, and scratching these areas often makes the condition worse. In most cases the dermatitis begins as a dry rash, but in some cases the eczema can become moist and 'weeping'. In severe cases it can become infected from scratching.

Outlook

There is no cure for eczema, but in most cases the condition improves with age. About 50% of children get better by the age of two years, and about 85% are better by five years of age. In the others, the condition usually improves somewhat with age, but can become chronic.

Management

Prevention

The first principle of management of eczema is to avoid aggravating factors—if these are known. Heat is a common aggravating factor, and children with eczema often prefer light clothing in which their skin feels cool. Some children find that the internal labels and seams of clothes cause irritation; in these cases, it can be helpful if clothes are worn inside out or if labels are carefully removed by unpicking them (without leaving any portion of the label behind to cause further irritation).

The first principle of management of eczema is to avoid aggravating factors.

Certain foods in the diet can aggravate eczema in some children; if known, these foods should be avoided.

Before swimming in chlorinated pools, children with eczema should have moisturiser applied to affected areas. After swimming, they should be immediately showered and more moisturiser should be carefully applied.

Treatment

Treatment of eczema usually consists of a combination of one or more of the following:

- moisturisers (such as 'Hydraderm');
- coal tar preparations; and
- cortisone ointments and creams.

Medical advice should be sought on the best combination for any particular child.

Technical terms used in this chapter

This chapter uses some technical terms as a 'shorthand' way of describing what happens with dermatitis. Most of these are explained in the text, but this list might also be helpful.

Acute
Something that has started only recently (perhaps in the last few hours)

Analgesics
Pain-killers

Chronic
Something that has been present for a relatively long time (perhaps weeks)

Hypersensitivity
An 'over-reaction' to something in the environment

Inflammation
An area of redness, heat, swelling, and pain; occurs in response to infection, irritation, or injury

Recurrent
Something that comes back again

Sign
Something that a parent or carer notices in a sick child (such as a rash)

Symptom
Something that the sick child complains about but other people cannot see (such as pain)

Severe cases of eczema sometimes require admission to hospital. A system of 'wet dressings' can be applied by nursing staff, and this can achieve quite dramatic improvements—even in severe cases.

Psoriasis

What is psoriasis?

Psoriasis (pronounced 'sor-RIE-a sis') is a chronic, itchy skin disease that can affect any part of the skin. The name of the disease comes from the Greek word for 'itch'.

Most cases develop between the ages of 15 and 35 years, but it can occur at any age. About 10–15% of cases occur in children who are under 10 years of age, and it occasionally occurs in infancy.

The cause is unknown, but it appears to run in families. In about one in three cases there is a family history of psoriasis.

Signs and symptoms

In a typical case of psoriasis, the skin becomes inflamed and thickened, with silvery skin scales over the inflamed areas. It is usually very itchy. Psoriasis can affect any part of the body—including the scalp, elbows, knees, and lower back.

In many cases, people with psoriasis notice new areas of inflammation about ten days after the skin has been cut, scratched, rubbed, or badly sunburnt. It seems that the condition might be related to abnormal attempts by the person's body to repair the skin. Physical and emotional stress can also trigger episodes of psoriasis. Flare-ups often occur in winter—perhaps as a result of lack of sunlight (which appears to improve psoriasis in summer).

Treatment

There is no cure for psoriasis. The goal is to minimise the inflammation and scaling of the skin.

Sunlight is often helpful in reducing inflammation in psoriasis, and synthetic vitamin D has been useful in helping some people. Special diets are not usually effective, but are occasionally helpful in some patients.

There is no cure for psoriasis; the goal is to minimise the inflammation and scaling of the skin.

Moisturising preparations can be useful to loosen scales and control itching. Anti-inflammatory preparations (such as coal tar and cortisone) are useful.

There are also some specific 'anti-psoriasis' preparations available (such as anthralin). However, these can cause problems if used inappropriately, and they should be used only with medical advice.

Ringworm

What is ringworm?

The term 'ringworm' (or 'tinea') is used to describe a fungal infection of the skin. The affected skin typically has a red border (like a ring) and the term 'ringworm' reflects the ancient belief that the dermatitis was caused by a burrowing worm under the skin. In fact, the Latin word *tinea* literally means 'gnawing worm'. We now know that the infection is caused by various sorts of fungus.

The infection can affect different parts of the body.

- If it occurs on the *trunk* it is properly called 'tinea corporis' (tinea of the body).
- If it occurs on the *head* it is properly called 'tinea capitis' (tinea of the scalp).
- If it occurs on the *feet* it is properly called 'tinea pedis' (tinea of the feet, or 'athlete's foot').

Signs and symptoms

As the name suggests, the dermatitis of 'ringworm' (or 'tinea') typically consists of a reddened area of skin with a darker-red margin. It can occur anywhere on the body, but the armpits, groins, scalp, and feet are common areas that are affected.

Tight shoes and damp socks increase the growth of the fungi.

The fungi that cause tinea like to grow in moist, closed environments. This is why tinea often occurs in the armpits, in the groins, or between the toes. Tight shoes and damp socks increase the growth of the fungi, and this is why the sports shoes of children ('gym boots') are especially likely to encourage the development of tinea pedis ('athlete's foot').

Spread and prevention

The fungi that cause the infection are carried on tiny fragments of skin that contaminate floors (including shower floors), mats, bed linen, clothes, shoes, and other surfaces.

Thorough daily washing and drying under the arms, in the groins, and between the toes can help to prevent tinea. However, excessive washing and scrubbing can damage the skin and increase the risk of infection.

Frequent changing of socks (and the use of anti-perspirant powder in socks) can be helpful in preventing tinea of the feet. Sweaty 'gym shoes' should be allowed to dry out completely in fresh air—not kept overnight in closed sports bags and put on again next day.

Thorough daily washing and drying ... can help to prevent tinea; however, excessive scrubbing can damage the skin and increase the risk of infection.

Treatment

Anti-fungal preparations (shampoos, paints, creams, etc.) are now readily available 'over the counter' from pharmacists. These should be used strictly as directed. It can take some time to eradicate the fungus from the deeper layers of the skin, and repeated treatments are usually necessary.

If the condition is severe or persistent, it might be necessary to use oral preparations (tablets) to get rid of the infection. These usually require a doctor's prescription.

Scabies

What is scabies?

The word 'scabies' comes from the Latin word for 'scratch'. It is caused by infection with a skin mite called *Sarcoptes scabei.* The female mite burrows into the skin and lays eggs. These hatch and the larvae move to the surface, develop into adult mites, and thus complete the life cycle.

A person usually has the infection for about a month before signs and symptoms become apparent. The mite is spread only by close personal contact—such as people living together or those in an institution. It affects people of all ages and is common among young children.

The mite is spread only by close personal contact—such as people living together or those in an institution.

Signs and symptoms

The mites, eggs, and larvae cause irritation of the skin and provoke intense itching. In some cases the 'burrows' of the female mite can be seen on the skin as fine, grey thread-like lines—typically in the webbing between the fingers or the toes. However, the intense itching and scratching usually causes a generalised redness and inflammation, and it is not possible to see the burrows. In most cases the dermatitis looks like eczema. In some cases the itching has been so intense that the dermatitis becomes infected with bacteria.

The diagnosis is usually made on the basis of a child having intense itching and scratching—especially of the hands and feet (although it can be anywhere on the body).

It is possible for mites to be spread from animals to humans—especially from dogs.

Treatment

Scabies is usually treated with an 'anti-scabies' insecticide—such as permethrin. This is available 'over the counter' from pharmacists. It should be applied from head to toe at bedtime, and then washed off in the morning. If new itchy areas develop later, a second treatment might be needed. However, insecticide preparations should not be repeatedly used without consulting a doctor.

All people in the household and any other close contacts should also be treated at the same time.

All people in the household and any other close contacts (including childcare contacts) should also be treated at the same time. In addition, on the same day of treatment, all clothing, bed linen, and towels should be washed in hot water and machine-dried.

Head lice

What are head lice?

Head lice, properly called *Pediculus humanus capitis*, are small, wingless, blood-sucking insects about 2–3 millimetres in length. Their colour varies from whitish-brown to reddish brown. They live only on the scalp of humans. If they are isolated from the human scalp, they die quickly (usually within 24 hours).

The lice are found on the hair itself, where they hold on with little claws, but they move to the scalp to feed (by blood-sucking). This causes itching of the scalp.

The eggs of the lice (often called 'nits') are laid within 1–2 centimetres of the scalp. They are firmly attached to the hair. They look like dandruff, but they cannot be brushed off.

Spread

Head lice do not have wings and they cannot jump. The lice are therefore spread from person to person *only* by direct hair-to-hair contact—such as occurs when playing, cuddling, or playing closely together.

The lice are spread from person to person only by direct hair-to-hair contact.

Although parents and carers are often appalled at the idea that their child might have head lice, it should be remembered that head lice live perfectly well on clean, healthy hair. Having head lice does not mean that a child is 'dirty'.

Finding head lice

The most important first step in treating and controlling head lice is to find them! The 'conditioner-and-comb' method is recommended. This should be performed regularly and carefully. Using this method once a week will detect any head lice early, and thus minimise the problem.

This is not a difficult task, but it does take time. Finding head lice does not require any special skills or training, but it does require patience! It can't be done in ten minutes just before bedtime. For children with long hair, the process can take 2–3 hours if it is to be done properly. Even with short hair, the process takes an hour. The Box on page 95 summarises the best way of detecting head lice.

Conditioner-and-comb method

To find head lice, parents and carers should follow the following steps.

1. Ensure that the child's hair is dry and untangled.
2. Comb hair conditioner (any type) through the child's hair. Aim to cover every hair with conditioner from root to tip. (The conditioner 'stuns' the lice and makes it difficult for them to hang onto the hair.)
3. Using a fine-tooth head-lice comb, comb sections of the hair carefully and thoroughly.
4. Wipe the conditioner from the comb onto a paper towel or tissue.
5. Look at the tissue and on the comb for any lice or eggs ('nits').
6. Repeat the combing for every part of the head at least five times.

Note: This process takes time. Patience and care are required.

Treating head lice

If head lice are detected with the above method, the head lice need to be treated. There are several options. These include:

- insecticides;
- frequent use of the 'conditioner-and-comb' method; or
- other methods.

Each of these is described below. Whichever method is chosen, there is no need to treat anything apart from the child's hair and pillowcase. There is no evidence that cleaning the child's clothing, the house, or a classroom makes any difference. The child's hair should be treated (as described below), and his or her pillowcase should be washed in hot water and machine-dried (using hot or warm setting).

Insecticide methods

There are several insecticide preparations for treating head lice. The product should be applied to all areas of the scalp and hair. All hairs should be coated from the roots to tips. If using lotions, apply the product to dry hair. If using shampoos, the hair should be wet, but this should be done with the least volume of water possible. The child's eyes should be covered while the treatment is being applied. The child can be asked to hold a towel against the eyes.

> A second treatment is needed to kill any eggs that hatch in the intervening week.

The preparation should be left on the hair for at least 20 minutes, and then washed out.

A second treatment is required after one week. This is because the insecticide does not kill all eggs, and a second treatment is therefore needed to kill any eggs that hatch in the intervening week.

Some head lice are resistant to certain insecticides. If this occurs, it is necessary to repeat the two treatments using a different type of insecticide.

Conditioner-and-comb method

The 'conditioner-and-comb' method (as described in the Box on page 95 for finding lice) can also be used as a treatment. This should be carried out every second day until there are no live lice found. This can be time-consuming, but the method is effective and it does avoid using insecticides on a child's head.

Other methods

There are various other methods available. These include essential oils of various types and electronic combs. However, there is little definite research on the value of these methods.

Prevention

There is no product available that prevents head lice occurring. As noted above, using the 'conditioner-and-comb' method once a week will detect any head lice early, and minimise the problem. Tying back long hair can help to prevent the spread of head lice.

The "conditioner-and-comb" method once a week will detect any head lice early, and minimise the problem.

Children with head lice should be kept away from school until treatment has commenced. A child can be treated one evening and return to school the next day, even if some eggs are still present.

Chapter 10

Fractures and Dislocations

Common in children

Younger children are at greater risk of injury than older children and adults. This is because:

- they have a poor understanding of risk and danger;
- they are unaware of their own limitations; and
- they are easily distracted.

Boys are twice as likely as girls to injure themselves.

There are, of course, many possible causes of injury in children. Falls are one of the most common—especially falls from playground equipment. Children aged 5–9 years are most likely to be affected. The most common injuries from playground equipment are fractures of the limbs, especially of the arms. Head injuries can also occur.

Framework of chapter

This chapter discusses musculoskeletal injuries, especially fractures and dislocations, under the following headings:

Musculoskeletal injuries

What are musculoskeletal injuries?

As the word suggests, the term 'musculoskeletal' refers to the muscles and skeleton of the body. The term 'musculoskeletal injury' thus includes any injury to the muscles and bones (and the associated tendons and ligaments that hold things together). These injuries include:

- bruises;
- tears, sprains, and strains;
- dislocations; and
- fractures (breaks).

Technical terms used in this chapter

This chapter uses some technical terms as a 'shorthand' way of describing what happens with injuries. Most of these are explained in the text, but this list might also be helpful.

Acute
Something that has started only recently (perhaps in the last few hours)

Analgesics
Pain-killers

Chronic
Something that has been present for a relatively long time (perhaps weeks)

Clavicle
The 'collarbone'—the prominent bone that runs from the centre of the chest to the shoulder.

Colles fracture
A fracture of the radius bone of the forearm, just above the wrist; usually with a typical 'dinner-fork' deformity

Deformity
Wrong shape—especially a 'bent' fractured bone

Displaced
Out of normal position (usually referring to a fractured bone end)

Femur
The long bone of the thigh

Fracture
A break in a bone; contrary to popular belief, a 'fracture' and a 'break' are exactly the same thing

Humerus
The long bone of the upper arm

Inflammation
An area of redness, heat, swelling, and pain; occurs in response to infection, irritation, or injury

(continued)

(continued)

Musculoskeletal
Something affecting the muscles and bones of the body

Patella
The knee cap

Radius
One of the two long bones of the forearm

Recurrent
Something that comes back again

Sign
Something that a parent or carer notices in a sick child (such as a rash)

Symptom
Something that the sick child complains about but other people cannot see (such as pain)

Tibia
The main long bone of the lower leg

Undisplaced
Still in normal position (usually referring to a fractured bone end)

Assessment of musculoskeletal injuries

If a child suffers a musculoskeletal injury, parents and carers should check the following things:

- general observation;
- blood supply;
- nerve supply; and
- pain.

General observation

The child's overall appearance should be checked for colour, consciousness, and general well-being. If there are no serious problems with the child's general appearance, the affected area should be examined for swelling, bruising, and deformity (wrong shape).

If the injury is on one side of the body, it is a good idea to check the other side and compare to see if there is any significant difference between the two in appearance and shape.

If there are any open wounds these should be treated (see Chapter 12, 'Wounds and Burns', page 115).

Blood supply

The blood supply to a limb can be damaged in significant trauma—for example, with some fractured bones. If there is any evidence that blood supply has been damaged, urgent medical attention is required.

The blood supply can be checked by feeling for a pulse. Although it is sometimes difficult to check for a pulse in the wrist or ankle of an injured child, parents and carers who know how to do this should attempt to do so. In addition, the overall colour and temperature of an injured limb gives a good indication of blood supply. The injured limb should therefore be checked to see if it is paler and/or cooler than the other side; the hand or foot is the best place to check for this. A test for 'capillary refill' of the fingers and/or toes is another good test of blood supply. This is described in the Box below.

Capillary refill on an injured limb

Step 1
Using a fingertip, the parent or carer presses firmly on the skin of a finger or toe. Firm pressure is maintained for five seconds.

Step 2
Remove the pressure and observe the child's skin. The area where pressure has been applied will be white.

Step 3
Watch to see how long the skin takes to become pink again. *The skin should return to a pink colour within two seconds.*

Nerve supply

Like the blood supply, the nerves to a limb can be damaged in significant trauma. Nerves do two things—they control movement and they supply sensation. Both of these can be checked. If there is any evidence that nerve supply has been damaged, urgent medical attention is required.

The child should be asked to move the fingers or toes on the injured limb. In less severe injuries, the movements of other joints can also be checked (the ankles and knees in the legs, and the wrists and elbows in the arms). The two sides should be compared. If the child is in pain, this might prevent much movement; however, an indication of movement can be obtained in most cases (especially in the fingers and toes).

> If there is any evidence that nerve supply has been damaged, urgent medical attention is required.

Parents and carers should also check for sensation. This is done by asking the child to close his or her eyes. The parent then lightly touches the child's hand or foot in different places and asks the child to say 'yes' whenever a touch is felt. The child should also be asked whether the touch feels 'normal' or whether it feels 'strange' (such as a 'pins-and-needles' sensation). The two sides should be checked and compared.

Pain

It is often difficult to get an accurate assessment of pain from a small child—because the child is often frightened and has difficulty in locating and describing the pain. However, an attempt should be made to find out precisely where any pain is felt by the child, and how bad it is. Any changes in the location or intensity of pain should be noted.

Sprains and strains

What are 'sprains' and 'strains'?

The terms 'sprain' and 'strain' are often used vaguely, and many people think that they are the same thing. In fact, a 'sprain' is an injury to a *joint* (where two bones meet), whereas a strain is an injury to a *muscle*.

A *sprained joint* usually follows a 'wrenching' injury—such as a twisted ankle. The twisting injury tears some of the attachments that hold the joint in position. This usually causes pain and swelling in and around the joint.

A sprain is an injury to a joint, whereas a strain is an injury to a muscle.

A *strained muscle* is overstretching of the fibres that make up a muscle. In severe cases, the muscle fibres can actually tear (a 'torn muscle'). This usually causes pain and tenderness in the area affected—especially on movement of the affected muscle.

Both sprains and strains are unusual in children under 10 years of age. This is because the bones around a joint are relatively 'soft' in young children, and the ligaments and tendons are relatively strong. If an injury occurs, younger children (less than 10 years of age) thus tend to get bruises and fractures, but not sprains and strains. As children become older, sprains and strains become more common.

Treatment

In the initial stages, the aim of treatment in sprains and strains is to minimise the inflammation in the affected area. This is achieved by following the routine of 'RICE'. These letters ('R-I-C-E') stand for:

- rest;
- ice;
- compression; and
- elevation.

The affected area should be rested, and ice should be applied. This is best done by putting an ice pack (or a 'cold pack' of some sort) on the area. A packet of frozen peas or corn makes a useful 'cold pack' because it can be easily moulded to the shape of the limb. There should be a cloth barrier between the skin and the 'cold pack'. The 'cold pack' should be be applied for 10–20 minutes (if the child will tolerate it for that long), and this should be repeated at least 3–4 times a day, sometimes more often.

A firm bandage (called a 'compression bandage') should then be applied. This should be firm enough to prevent swelling, but not so tight that it affects blood and nerve supply to the limb.

The affected area should be elevated (again to prevent swelling).

This 'RICE' routine should be continued for about 48 hours. After that it is unlikely that any significant swelling will occur. Then the treatment is changed to encourage circulation to the area (to help healing). This is done with warmth, massage, and movement.

Fractures

What is a fracture?

Some people talk about 'fractured' bones and 'broken' bones as though they were different things. In fact, there is no difference: a fracture is a 'break', and a 'break' is a fracture.

Fractures can be minor or severe. Some are just 'bends' in the bone—like a bent green stick; in fact, these are known as 'greenstick fractures'. Others are more severe and involve a definite break on one or both sides of the bone. In severe injuries, there can be a wound in the skin over the fracture; this is commonly called a 'compound' or 'open' fracture.

First aid for a fracture

To provide first aid for a fracture, the steps described in the Box below should be taken.

First aid for a fracture

In providing first aid for a fracture, the following steps should be taken:

- stop any bleeding if present (by applying pressure);
- immobilise the fracture and splint in a comfortable position;
- apply icepack to area (if possible);
- provide pain relief (such as paracetamol); and
- transport to hospital or doctor.

To immobilise the fracture a variety of first-aid 'splints' can be used. Some of the possibilities include a rolled-up newspaper (and bandage), a flat piece of wood (and bandage), or a flat piece of firm plastic (and bandage). In many cases, the easiest way to immobilise the fracture is simply to support the injured limb on a pillow and let the child find a comfortable position.

Common and important fractures in children

Fractured clavicle

The clavicle is the 'collarbone'—the prominent bone that runs from the centre of the chest (just below the throat) to the shoulder. A fractured clavicle is relatively common in children. It usually results from a fall on an outstretched arm, but it can occur from a direct blow to the area.

Because the clavicle is so easy to see and feel, parents and carers can often diagnose this fracture themselves. In some cases it is possible to see a deformity in the clavicle. In other cases there is no obvious deformity but it is possible to run fingertips along the bone and feel a deformity (or produce pain when the fracture site is touched).

> Virtually all fractured clavicles heal well with no problems.

In almost all cases, a fractured clavicle is not serious. This is especially the case in children; virtually all fractured clavicles heal well with no problems. Medical assistance is required if there is significant deformity or if the fracture is very close to the shoulder. Otherwise, the treatment is simply a sling and painkillers (as required) until the fracture heals.

The discomfort usually goes away within about ten days (often sooner than this in younger children, who have 'soft' fast-healing bones), and the fracture usually heals in about three weeks. It is usually possible to feel a small lump over the fracture site for several weeks (or even months). This is called 'callus'. It is a normal part of the healing process and usually goes away with time.

Fractures in children

This portion of the text discusses common and important fractures in children. The following are discussed:

Fractured humerus

The humerus is the long bone of the upper arm. If children fall on an outstretched arm (from playground equipment, for example), they can sustain a fracture in the lower third of the humerus (just above the elbow). This is called a 'supra-condylar fracture of the humerus'. It produces a large amount of swelling around and above the elbow. The child is usually in extreme pain.

This sort of fracture is significant because there are important nerves and arteries in this region, and they can be damaged by the fractured bones—especially if the fractured bone ends are moved around. It is therefore very important that parents and carers do *not* try to move the child's arm or elbow in any way. If the child prefers to have the elbow straight, it should be left straight; if the child prefers to have the elbow bent, it should be left bent. The injured arm should be gently supported and the child should be taken to hospital as soon as possible. Because the child is usually in so much pain and because the fracture is dangerous, an ambulance is the best option.

It is very important that parents and carers do *not* try to move the child's arm or elbow in any way.

Colles fracture

A Colles (pronounced 'KOLL-ees') fracture affects the radius bone of the forearm, just above the wrist. It is a relatively common fracture and is usually caused by a child falling on an outstretched arm.

A Colles fracture produces a typical 'dinner-fork deformity' in the forearm and wrist. This term describes the shape of the deformity from side on—it looks like a dinner fork viewed from the side.

A variation on a typical Colles fracture is a minor crack in the lower radius with no deformity. In this case the wrist is painful and often swollen—but remains straight.

A child with a suspected Colles fracture should be taken for an X-ray. If the fracture has the classical 'dinner-fork deformity' this will have to be put back into place. This requires an anaesthetic (local or general), followed by manipulation of the fracture by a doctor. The child then goes home in a cast—usually extending from below the elbow to the fingers. The fracture takes about six weeks to heal.

A Colles fracture produces a typical "dinner-fork deformity" in the forearm and wrist.

Fractured femur

The femur is the long bone of the thigh. In older children and adolescents, the femur is a large, strong bone. This means that a fracture of the femur requires significant impact—such as falling off a roof or a horse, or being involved in a motor-bike or car accident. In younger children, especially pre-school children, a fracture of the femur can occur with a relatively trivial injury—such as tripping over when running.

In older children and adolescents, a fractured femur can be associated with quite severe internal blood loss.

In older children and adolescents, a fractured femur can be associated with quite severe internal blood loss, but this is not a problem with younger children.

The fracture should be immobilised. If the person is wearing tight trousers, these should be left in position because they help to hold the fracture in place and minimise internal bleeding. In older children and adolescents, the person's thighs should be bandaged or strapped together to act as a splint. However, in younger children this can cause severe pain and it is not necessary to splint the legs together; the leg should simply be left in a position of comfort.

A person with a fractured femur should obviously be transported to a hospital for expert assessment.

'Toddler's fracture'

A so-called 'toddler's fracture' is a fracture of the tibia (the main long bone of the lower leg). The fracture is undisplaced (still in normal position) and spiral-shaped (like a spiral staircase).

Next day the child typically refuses to walk on the affected leg.

A typical 'toddler's fracture' occurs when a small child has a fall when running. The child might be distressed at the time, but then he or she appears to recover and goes on with relatively normal activities. However, on the next day the child typically refuses to walk on the affected leg. When the child is taken to a doctor or hospital, an X-ray shows the typical fracture (although sometimes the fracture can be difficult to see).

The fracture heals well, usually without any complications.

Dislocations

What is a dislocation?

The term 'dislocation' means that the bones in a joint are out of alignment. All joints of the body consist of a junction of two bones. These are held in place by various surrounding tissues—including a 'capsule' around the joint, ligaments, and muscles.

The term "dislocation" means that the bones in a joint are out of alignment.

If an injury causes the ends of the bones in a joint to be out of alignment, this is called a 'dislocation'. In a 'pure' dislocation, the bones are not broken—although a person can sometimes suffer a combined fracture and dislocation in a joint.

Sometimes the dislocation goes back into place by itself, but usually the bones have to be put back into correct alignment by a doctor or nurse.

Common and important dislocations in children

Pulled elbow

A 'pulled elbow' is a dislocation of a relatively unstable part of the elbow joint. The condition tends to occur in children under five years of age—mostly about 2–3 years of age.

A 'pulled elbow' commonly occurs when a small child is being swung around by the arms. The child might suddenly complain of pain in the elbow; alternatively, the child might not complain but simply refuse to use the affected arm. Any attempt to examine the sore elbow or move the arm is likely to make the child scream with pain.

A "pulled elbow" commonly occurs when a small child is being swung around by the arms.

The problem is not serious. The dislocation affects the head of the radius bone—one of the two bones of the forearm—and the dislocated bone can be easily put back into place by a doctor or trained nurse. There are no long-term effects.

Dislocated patella

The patella is the knee cap. When a person walks or runs, the patella slides up and down in a 'track' over the lower part of the femur (thigh bone). Sometimes the patella 'tracks' badly and slides off sideways. It ends up on the 'outside' of the knee as a dislocated patella. Many people mistakenly believe that this is a 'dislocated knee'. A dislocated knee is actually a very rare condition that occurs only with massive trauma (such as a severe car accident).

A dislocated patella occurs most commonly in adolescent girls, and is especially likely to occur when they are doing twisting movements of the knee with the foot fixed in position—such as when dancing or playing netball.

A dislocated patella occurs most commonly in adolescent girls.

The condition is not serious, but it can sometimes cause quite severe pain. The first step in treatment is to put the patella back in position. This requires analgesia (pain-killers) and manipulation of the patella by a doctor. After the patella has been put back in position the patient needs to be X-rayed and assessed by an expert. The condition does tend to be recurrent (that is, it does tend to happen again).

Problems with casts

Any child who has a cast (plaster or fibreglass) applied to a limb should be closely observed in the hours and days following application of the cast. The child's limb should be watched for any evidence of:

- swelling;
- poor circulation;
- pressure on nerves; or
- pain.

Swelling

If there is any sign of swelling in the affected limb, the arm or leg should be elevated. If the swelling persists after elevation the child should be taken back to the doctor or hospital. It might be necessary to remove the cast to relieve the pressure.

Poor circulation

As noted above (see 'Blood supply', page 99), the blood supply can be checked by:

- feeling for a pulse;
- checking for paleness in the hand or foot;
- checking for decreased temperature in the hand or foot; and
- checking for 'capillary refill' (see Box, page 100).

If there is any sign of poor circulation, the child should be taken back to the doctor or hospital.

Pressure on nerves

As noted above (see 'Nerve supply', page 100), the nerves to a limb can be checked by:

- asking the child to move the fingers or toes on the injured limb;
- touching the hand or foot and testing for sensation; and
- asking the child whether there are any 'pins and needles'.

If there is any sign of pressure on nerves, the child should be taken back to the doctor or hospital.

Pain

Although a fracture is painful, the pain should decrease significantly once the fracture has been treated and a cast has been applied. The pain should continue to decrease over the next few days.

If the pain persists, or becomes worse, the child should be taken back to the doctor or hospital.

Chapter 11

Head Injuries

Introduction

Most parents and carers are understandably worried if a child suffers an injury to the head. However, they can be reassured that minor injuries to the head are common in childhood, and that the overwhelming majority are not serious. The problem is to know how to recognise the more serious head injuries from among the 'everyday' events that have no significant consequences.

This chapter provides guidance to parents and carers in evaluating head injuries and deciding when to seek medical assistance. The chapter discusses head injuries according to the framework shown in the Box below.

Framework of chapter

This chapter discusses head injuries under the following headings:

Potentially serious head injuries

Minor head injuries are common in childhood. Minor 'everyday' knocks to the head—such as tripping over and striking the head, or walking into a door and being momentarily 'stunned'—are unlikely to cause any problems.

Nearly all serious head injuries are associated with a really significant traumatic blow to the head. These are usually 'high-velocity' blows—such as occur in a car accident, or falling to the ground from an upstairs window, or being hit in the head with a flying cricket ball. There is no need to be especially worried unless there is a history of a really significant traumatic event. In other words, in assessing a potentially serious head injury, parents and carers should make every effort to find out *exactly* what happened—with a view to discovering whether there has been any dangerous, high-velocity impact.

Nearly all serious head injuries are associated with a really significant traumatic blow to the head.

Technical terms used in this chapter

This chapter uses some technical terms as a 'shorthand' way of describing what happens with head injuries. Most of these are explained in the text, but this list might also be helpful.

Acute
Something that has started only recently (perhaps in the last few hours)

Amnesia
A loss of memory

Analgesics
Pain-killers

Chronic
Something that has been present for a relatively long time (perhaps weeks)

Concussion
A temporary loss of brain function after a head injury

Dizziness
Feeling 'faint' and 'light-headed'

Recurrent
Something that comes back again

Seizure
A 'fit' or convulsion

Sign
Something that a parent or carer notices in a sick child (such as a rash)

Symptom
Something that the sick child complains about but other people cannot see (such as pain)

Syndrome
A collection of signs and symptoms

Vertigo
Things in the environment seeming to go 'round and round' the head.

Apart from finding out the exact nature of the actual injury, parents and carers should also find out (if possible) whether the child *lost consciousness*—and if so, for how long. This is likely to require reports from reliable witnesses who saw what happened. Any loss of consciousness that is longer than 'momentary' is potentially significant.

Any loss of consciousness that is longer than "momentary" is potentially significant.

Finally, if there is any sign of *amnesia* (loss of memory) in the child, parents and carers should be more concerned. In most cases, if amnesia is present following a loss of consciousness, the child will not be able to remember the exact moment of the injury. The child's recall of events is likely to be quite good up until a certain time *before* the actual moment of the injury—perhaps several minutes before. The child is likely to say something like: 'The last thing I remember is …'.

Putting all of this together, in assessing whether a head injury is potentially serious, parents and carers should find out:

- *exactly* what happened;
- whether there was any *loss of consciousness*; and
- whether there is any evidence of *amnesia*.

The Box below summarises the indications of a potentially serious head injury.

Indications of a potentially serious head injury

A head injury is more likely to be serious if:

- the child has fallen from a significant height (for example, the upper storey of a two-storey house);
- the child has been injured in a motor vehicle accident or bike accident;
- the child has been involved in a competitive 'high-velocity' sporting activity (such as football or cricket);
- the child definitely lost consciousness after the blow (for any longer than a 'momentary' loss of consciousness); and
- the child is suffering from amnesia (loss of memory) after the event.

Concussion

What is concussion?

The term 'concussion' refers to a temporary loss of brain function after a head injury. Concussion usually, but not always, follows a loss of consciousness. Amnesia (loss of memory) can occur, but it is rarely permanent.

The most common head injury that causes concussion is, of course, a direct blow to the head. But concussion can also be due to sudden 'acceleration and deceleration' forces acting on the soft brain inside the skull—as can occur when a speeding car stops suddenly in a crash and the brain 'bounces around' in the head.

Concussion is a temporary loss of brain function after a head injury.

Grades of concussion

Most cases of concussion in children are not serious. In the majority of cases the child can be cared for at home after being assessed by a doctor.

Doctors assess concussion by looking for three main features in the patient:

- *confusion* (unsure of time and/or place);
- *amnesia* (a loss of memory of the injury); and
- *loss of consciousness* (even briefly).

By looking at these three main features, doctors 'grade' the concussion. The guidelines in the Box below show how this is done. Parents and carers can also make a reasonable judgment about the severity of concussion by looking for these three main features. If there is any doubt about the child's condition, he or she should be taken to a doctor or hospital for a proper assessment.

Post-concussion syndrome

The term 'syndrome' refers to a collection of signs and symptoms. It is expected that children will have *some* signs and symptoms after they suffer concussion (such as those described above).

Grades of concussion

Three main features

Doctors assess concussion after a head injury by looking at three main features:

- *Confusion:* Is the child 'confused' after the head injury? (Does the child know where he or she is, or what day it is?)
- *Amnesia:* Is the child suffering from loss of memory of the injury?
- *Loss of consciousness:* Did the child suffer any loss of consciousness (even briefly)?

The answers to these questions provide three grades of concussion (as follows).

Grade 1 concussion ('Yes' to the first, but 'no' to the other two)

- *Confusion:* The child *is* confused.
- *Amnesia:* The child does *not* have amnesia.
- *Loss of consciousness:* The child did *not* lose consciousness.

Grade 2 concussion ('Yes' to the first two, but 'no' to the last)

- *Confusion:* The child *is* confused.
- *Amnesia:* The child *does* have amnesia.
- *Loss of consciousness:* The child did *not* lose consciousness.

Grade 3 concussion ('Yes' to all three)

- *Confusion:* The child *is* confused.
- *Amnesia:* The child *does* have amnesia.
- *Loss of consciousness:* The child *did* lose consciousness.

Assessment

The more severe grades of concussion obviously require more detailed assessment and observation.

Note: If there is any doubt about the child's condition, the child should be taken to a doctor or hospital for a proper assessment.

However, these should clear up within a few days. If signs and symptoms persist for longer than a few days, this is called 'post-concussion syndrome'.

The signs and symptoms of post-concussion syndrome can include:

- headaches;
- difficulty with concentration;
- irritability;
- memory problems;
- dizziness (feeling 'faint' and 'light-headed'); and
- vertigo (things in the environment seeming to go 'round and round' the head).

Post-concussion syndrome is less common in children than in adults. However, it *can* occur in children, and parents and carers should be alert for any *ongoing* problems after their child has suffered concussion. If they are worried, parents should take the child to see a doctor to ensure that there is nothing more serious going on.

There is no specific treatment for post-concussion syndrome—other than rest and time.

There is no specific treatment for post-concussion syndrome—other than rest and time. It usually takes 1–3 months for all ill-effects to go away. The headaches can last longer than this. It might be necessary to have discussions with teachers and sports coaches with a view to having the child's usual school and sporting routines changed until the child makes a full recovery.

Post-traumatic seizures

Seizures (or 'fits') after a head injury are more common in children than in adults; however, they are usually less serious in children.

In children, the occurrence of a seizure after a head injury does not necessarily mean that the head injury is very serious. Nor does it mean that the child will develop epilepsy.

However, although a seizure after a head injury is not necessarily serious, parents and carers should still take the child to a doctor or hospital for a full assessment to rule out a more serious problem—such as a fractured skull or internal bleeding inside the skull.

Management

Initial assessment

If a child suffers a head injury, parents and carers should first make a general assessment of the child's overall well-being. In particular they should check to see whether there is any sign of:

- *confusion* (unsure of time and place);
- *amnesia* (loss of memory of injury); or
- *loss of consciousness* (even briefly).

As well as noting these things on an initial examination, parents and carers should also observe these signs and symptoms over a period of time (minutes to hours). Any deterioration requires urgent medical assessment.

As previously noted, it is important to find out exactly what happened (see 'Indications of a potentially serious head injury' in the Box on page 109). If there are any of the features of a potentially serious head injury (as listed in that Box), the child should be taken to a doctor or hospital.

The child's head should be examined to see if there is any bruising, swelling, or cuts. If there is any bleeding, pressure should be applied until the bleeding stops. Cuts to the scalp can be frightening because they bleed profusely; in most cases the cut is found to be minor—even if there is quite a lot of initial bleeding. A more serious cut obviously requires medical attention.

Cuts to the scalp can be frightening because they bleed profusely; in most cases the cut is found to be minor.

The child's neck should also be gently checked. If there is any doubt, it is best to assume that the child has a neck injury. The neck should be kept straight and gently supported.

Managing an unconscious child

If the child remains unconscious, the head injury is obviously very serious and urgent medical attention is required. An emergency ambulance should be called (or sent for) immediately.

While waiting for expert assistance, a parent or carer should remain in attendance at all times. The child should never be left alone.

If there is a possibility of a neck injury, it is generally best not to move the child at all. However, if the child's breathing is obstructed, or if there is any sign of possible vomiting, the child should be gently moved onto his or her side while carefully supporting the head and neck (and avoiding any twisting movements).

In extreme cases, CPR (cardiopulmonary resuscitation) might be required. For more on CPR, see Chapter 13, 'Emergency Care', page 123.

Three common myths

There are three common 'myths' about managing head injuries in children.

The first is a belief that analgesics ('painkillers') should not be given to a child after a head injury. This is false. If a child has a headache or other pain after a head injury, a dose of paracetamol will help to relieve the child's pain and distress. Pain-killers will do no harm at all; in fact they are likely to make the child more comfortable and cooperative.

Pain-killers will do no harm at all; in fact they are likely to make the child more comfortable and cooperative.

The second 'myth' is that some people believe that a child should not be allowed to sleep after a head injury. Again, this is false. If a child is tired and wants to sleep there is no reason for keeping that child awake. In fact, if the child is kept awake unnecessarily, this will make the child irritable and uncooperative—and this irritability will make assessment more difficult later on. A child should therefore be allowed to sleep if he or she wishes to do so. If parents and carers are worried, the most important test is whether the child can be woken up—not whether the child wants to go to sleep!

Thirdly, some people believe that a 'cold pack' should not be applied to a head injury. There is no clear evidence for this belief. If a cold pack is required—to minimise swelling or to control bleeding—there is no proven reason for not doing so.

Final word

This chapter began by reassuring parents and carers that most head injuries in children are not serious. However, although it is true that most head injuries do not cause significant problems, parents and carers should 'follow their instincts' in deciding whether to seek medical help. If parents and carers are worried, they should take the child to a doctor or hospital.

Chapter 12

Wounds and Burns

Types of wounds

A wound is a break in the skin. Various words are used to describe different sorts of wounds—depending on the appearance of the wound and the nature of the injury that caused the break in the skin. Some common terms that are used to describe wounds are as follows:

- a *contusion:* a bruise (from the Latin word for 'thump');
- an *abrasion:* a scraping or rubbing injury (from the Latin word for 'scrape');
- a *laceration:* a cut or tear (from the Latin word for 'torn');
- an *avulsion:* pulling-off or tearing-away of the skin and underlying tissues (from the Latin word for 'pluck off' or 'pull away');
- a *puncture wound:* a penetrating wound made by a sharp point—such as a sharp knife or needle (from the Latin word for 'prick' or 'penetrate'); and
- a *bite:* a wound made by the teeth of an animal (including human).

In many cases, a single incident can produce several types of wounds. For example, a child who falls from a bike might have a contusion (bruise), an abrasion (scraping of the skin), and a laceration (tear of the skin).

First aid

Wounds are common in children. Virtually every child will suffer a minor wound of some sort at some time. It is therefore a good idea for all parents and carers to have some basic first-aid training. They should also have a simple first-aid kit in the home for dressing and bandaging minor wounds. Training courses in first aid are usually available in most centres.

Framework of chapter

This chapter discusses wounds under the following headings:

Minor wounds

Most wounds are not serious. In the majority of cases, parents and carers can manage small wounds themselves without assistance—especially if they have had some basic first-aid training.

The wound should be cleaned with soap and water. There is no need for antiseptic solutions. The wound should then be gently dried, and a dressing applied.

After treating all wounds (no matter how minor), parents and carers should consider:

- whether the wound should be assessed by an expert—especially if there is concern about cosmetic appearance (such as wounds on the face); and
- whether the child is adequately immunised against tetanus—because even relatively trivial wounds (especially puncture wounds) can cause tetanus.

Major wounds

Controlling bleeding

If a wound is bleeding freely, the first priority is to stop the bleeding. The steps shown in the Box below should be followed. These steps are explained in greater detail in the text that follows.

Control of bleeding

If a wound is bleeding freely, the following steps should be followed.

- Lie the child down.
- Elevate the wounded part of the body (arm, leg, head).
- Apply firm pressure to the wound with a clean dressing (or with your own hand in an emergency).
- Apply a firm bandage.
- Reinforce as necessary (but do not remove bottom layer of dressings already applied).
- Arrange for medical or nursing assistance to repair wound.

Technical terms used in this chapter

This chapter uses some technical terms as a 'shorthand' way of describing what happens with wounds. Most of these are explained in the text, but this list might also be helpful.

Abrasion
a scraping or rubbing injury

Acute
Something that has started only recently (perhaps in the last few hours)

Amputation
Cutting-off of part of the body

Avulsion
Pulling-off or tearing-away of the skin and underlying tissues

Chronic
Something that has been present for a relatively long time (perhaps weeks)

Contusion
A bruise

Epistaxis
A nosebleed

Laceration
A cut or tear

Sign
Something that a parent or carer notices in a sick child (such as a rash)

Symptom
Something that the sick child complains about but other people cannot see (such as pain)

The child should be instructed to lie down, and the wounded area should be elevated. These steps help to decrease the circulation of blood to the area—thus diminishing the bleeding.

Firm pressure should then be applied to the bleeding wound. If a clean dressing or cloth is available, this should be used to apply pressure. In an emergency, firm pressure should be applied directly with the carer's fingers or hands. Firm pressure usually stops most bleeding.

> Firm pressure usually stops most bleeding.

The wound should then have several layers of bandage applied to maintain pressure. If the bleeding seeps through the bandage, further layers of bandage should be applied over the top of the existing layers. If the blood continues to seep through, all bandages and dressing should be removed (except the bottom layer next to the wound), and more dressings and bandage should be applied directly over the wound. It is important not to remove the bottom layer (next to the wound) because the wound might have started to clot, and this clot might be pulled off if the bottom layer of a dressing is disturbed.

Once the bleeding has been controlled, arrangements should be made to have the wound repaired by a doctor or nurse.

Checking for other injuries

If a child has a more serious wound (or multiple wounds), there is always the possibility that the child has also suffered other injuries that are not immediately obvious. If a wound is bleeding profusely, control of the bleeding takes priority (as described above). However, if the child is not bleeding profusely (or if bleeding has already been controlled), parents and carers should check for other injuries. To do this they should follow the steps in the Box below.

Seeking further assistance

After bleeding has been controlled and the child has been checked for other injuries, medical assistance will usually be required for the further management of major wounds. Depending on the nature and extent of the wound, the child might need to be taken to a doctor, or an ambulance might be required.

As noted above, parents and carers should be especially careful to ensure:

- that the child is adequately immunised against tetanus; and
- that any wounds that might cause cosmetic concern (such as on the face) are properly cared for by an expert.

Checking for other injuries

If the child is not bleeding profusely (or if bleeding has already been controlled), parents and carers should check for other injuries. To do this they should take the following steps.

1. Check what happened

It is important to find out exactly what happened. This will provide clues to other possible injuries.

2. Check overall appearance

The child's overall appearance and well-being should be checked. Parents should check the child's colour and level of consciousness. The rest of the child's body should then be gently examined for any signs of other wounds or injuries (such as a fracture).

3. Check the circulation to hands and feet

Circulation to the hands and feet can be checked by:

- feeling for a pulse;
- checking for paleness in the hand or foot;
- checking for decreased temperature in the hand or foot; and
- checking for 'capillary refill' (see Box, Chapter 10, page 100).

4. Check the nerve supply to hands and feet

The nerve supply to the hands and feet can be checked by:

- asking the child to move the fingers or toes on the injured limb;
- touching the hand or foot and testing for sensation; and
- asking the child whether there are any strange feelings in the fingers or toes (such as 'tingling' or 'pins and needles').

Closing a wound

There are several different methods for 'closing' a wound. In most cases, parents and carers do not have to know the details of exactly how this is done. However, even if the wound is closed by a doctor or nurse, parents and carers are often responsible for 'after-care' of the repaired wound after the child has come home. They will therefore be interested to know how the wound has been closed. The following methods are commonly used.

- *Tissue glue:* This is similar to 'super glue'. It is often used in minor wounds to avoid the use of sutures. The glue 'disappears' of its own accord after a while (several days).
- *Steristrips:* These are little strips of adhesive material that are applied across the wound to hold the edges together. They 'drop off' after a while (days or weeks).
- *Sutures:* Sutures (or 'stitches') are used for wounds that cannot be held together by other means. The sutures used in skin wounds usually have to be removed 5–10 days later, depending on the location of the wound.

Nosebleeds

The technical name for a nosebleed is 'epistaxis'. Most nosebleeds are not due to trauma, and this topic might therefore seem out of place in a discussion of 'wounds'. However, it is convenient to discuss nosebleeds while we are discussing control of bleeding.

The child's head should be tilted *forwards*—not backwards, as many people believe.

The most important thing to know is that the child's head should be tilted *forwards*—not backwards, as many people believe. If the child's head is tilted backwards, the bleeding will simply continue, with the blood going back down to the child's throat. However, if the head is tilted forwards and the forward flow of blood is blocked (as described below), the 'back pressure' helps to put pressure on the bleeding point inside the nose.

To control a nosebleed, the following steps should be taken.

- Sit the child up with the head tilted forwards (so the blood is running out of the nostril).
- Using the thumb and forefinger, pinch the soft part of the child's nose (below the bony part) for at least 10 minutes.
- Remove thumb and finger and see if the bleeding resumes.
- If it does resume, repeat the procedure once or twice. If the bleeding lasts more than about 30 minutes, seek medical assistance.
- When bleeding stops, tell the child to avoid blowing his or her nose.

Placing a cold pack on the back of the child's neck will not do any harm—although there is no evidence that it does any good!

Amputations

If a part of the body (such as the end of a finger, for example) is completely amputated, it is important that parents and carers know what to do. Proper first-aid treatment of these injuries can make the difference between success and failure in attempting to re-attach the amputated part. The Box on page 120 lists the steps that should be taken.

First-aid for an amputation

Proper first-aid treatment of amputations can make the difference between success and failure in attempting to re-attach the amputated part. The following steps should be taken.

1. First treat the child

The first priority is treatment of the child. Bleeding should be controlled with elevation and firm pressure (see Box on 'Control of bleeding', page 116).

2. Looking after the amputated part

The amputated part should be retrieved. It should then be looked after as follows.

- Wrap the amputated part in a clean, damp cloth—such as gauze or a clean handkerchief. The cloth should be damp, *not* soaking wet.
- Place in a sealed container (such as a plastic food container).
- Place the container in an ice bucket or portable fridge (such as an 'Esky').

Note that the amputated part is not placed in direct contact with water or ice.

3. Transfer to appropriate expert medical facility

It is important to have the amputated part re-attached as soon as possible. It is therefore sensible to arrange for the child and the amputated part to be taken to a hospital where plastic surgery can be performed. Unless the child is bleeding profusely or requires care for other serious injuries, time should not be wasted by going to medical clinics or small hospitals where such surgery is not performed.

Dental trauma

As with amputations, first aid is very important if a child loses a tooth. If a child's tooth is retrieved, looked after, and then replaced promptly, it is likely to survive.

Parents and carers should first ascertain whether the tooth is a primary tooth (a 'milk tooth') or a secondary tooth (a 'permanent tooth'). If it is a primary tooth, it is *not* replaced. Only permanent teeth are replaced.

The tooth should be retrieved and washed gently in milk or clean water. Do *not* scrub the tooth because this can damage the fine fibres beside the root that assist the tooth to re-attach. The tooth should then be placed in milk and transported with the child to a dentist or doctor as soon as possible.

If expert attention from a dentist is unlikely to be available within a reasonable time (for example, an hour), parents and carers should carefully replace the tooth in its socket. The tooth should be gently washed in milk (*not* scrubbed vigorously) and then replaced—ensuring that the tooth is replaced in the correct socket and the right way around. It can be held in place with a moulded piece of aluminium foil, and the child should be given a small piece of clean gauze or cloth to bite on gently (to hold the replaced tooth and aluminium foil in position). Expert attention from a dentist should then be obtained as soon as possible.

Animal bites

Common, but preventable

Dog bites are one of the most common causes of preventable serious injury in small children. Toddlers should never be left alone in the vicinity of dogs or allowed to get close to a dog.

Any dog should be assumed to be a danger to small children. Even the friendly family pet is liable to snap if a child puts his or her face close to the dog's head.

Management

The major problem with animal bites is infection. All animal bites (including human bites) are infected, and antibiotics are usually required. Tetanus infection is also a risk.

If the wound is minor, it should be cleaned thoroughly with soap and water. Any bleeding should be controlled with pressure, and the wound should be covered with a dry dressing. If the wound is more severe, elevation and a pressure bandage might be required to control the bleeding.

All animal bites are infected, and antibiotics are usually required.

The child should then be taken to a doctor for antibiotics and review of tetanus immunisation. An ambulance might be required in severe injuries.

Burns

Burns and scalds

Burns and scalds cause similar injuries, but they are not exactly the same thing. A scald is actually an injury caused by hot liquid, whereas a burn is an injury caused by dry heat. However, most people simply talk about 'burns'.

Depth of burns

The severity of a burn depends on how deep it is. Burns are usually described as 'superficial', 'partial thickness', or 'full thickness'. The skin has three layers, and these descriptions of the depth of a burn correspond to these three layers. In simple terms:

- a superficial burn affects only the outermost layer of the skin;
- a partial-thickness burn affects the outermost layer *and* the tissue of the skin immediately under this layer; and
- a full-thickness burn affects *all* layers of the skin down to the underlying fat, muscle, and bone.

The deeper burns are obviously more significant. Some superficial burns can be managed at home, but deeper burns usually require medical or nursing care.

First aid for burns

First aid treatment for burns is important because it can stop the burning process and prevent ongoing damage. Even after the initial source of burning heat has been removed, the cells in the skin continue to be damaged by an ongoing internal burning process—like a 'pressure cooker' in each of the little cells. It is very important that this burning process be stopped as soon as possible. This is achieved by the steps shown in the Box on page 122.

There are several important things that should be noted in the steps outlined in the Box.

The first is that the burning process *must* be stopped before seeking medical advice. Some parents and carers believe that they must get the child to a doctor or hospital as soon as possible.

First-aid treatment for burns

It is very important that the burning process be stopped as soon as possible. The following steps should be taken:

- Hold the burnt area under cold running water. Do *not* use ice.
- Continue for 10–20 minutes until the area no longer feels warm.
- Remove any clothing from the burnt area—as long as it is not stuck to the wound.
- Cover with 'ordinary' kitchen cling film wrap. Do *not* apply any creams or lotions.
- Elevate the burnt area.
- Keep the child warm once the burn is covered.
- Give paracetamol.
- Seek medical advice.

They therefore do nothing about the burn itself; instead, they immediately set off for help. However, in the time that it takes to get a doctor or hospital, more damage is being done by the ongoing internal burning process. It is much better to stop the burning process—before seeking additional help.

The second important thing to be noted in the Box above is the use of 'ordinary' kitchen cling film wrap as a dressing. This is an excellent dressing for burns, and is *strongly recommended.* Cling wrap has two significant benefits.

- It stops air getting to the burn. Air causes pain in burns. By sealing the burn off from air, the child's pain is significantly decreased.
- It is transparent. When the child is eventually seen by a doctor or nurse, a cling-film dressing allows trained staff to examine the burn without putting the child through the discomfort of removing the dressing.

Parents and carers should *always* wrap a burn in cling wrap once they have stopped the burning process with cold running water.

Chapter 13

Emergency Care

Introduction

This chapter discusses the emergency care of some potentially life-threatening situations involving children. It is not possible for the chapter to cover everything that would be covered in a course on emergency first aid. For more information on emergency first aid, parents and carers are encouraged to undertake an accredited first-aid course.

Framework of chapter

This chapter discusses the emergency care of some potentially life-threatening situations involving children. The chapter discusses the following:

- Allergic reactions (this page)
- Seizures (page 126)
- Resuscitation (page 129)

Allergic reactions

Anaphylaxis

Minor common allergic reactions that produce skin rashes were mentioned in Chapter 3 (see 'Urticaria', page 36). In some cases, allergic reactions can become more serious. The most severe reactions are called 'anaphylaxis' (pronounced 'an-a-FILL-ax-is'), and the reaction is called an 'anaphylactic reaction' (pronounced 'an-a-FILL-act-ik'). These anaphylactic reactions can be life-threatening.

Any child can have an anaphylactic reaction—even if he or she has not reacted in this way previously. However, in most cases, the body needs prior exposure to a substance to develop the antibodies that lead to an anaphylactic reaction. For example, in the past a child might have developed only a localised swelling in response to a bee sting; however, on a subsequent occasion, the child might have an anaphylactic reaction in response to a bee sting.

Every child who is known to have a potential anaphylactic reaction should have emergency medications on hand and a management plan in readiness.

The reaction usually appears rapidly—within seconds or minutes after exposure to the substance to which the child is allergic. In rare cases, the reaction can be somewhat delayed. Because the reaction is usually so rapid, every child who is known to have a potential anaphylactic reaction should have emergency medications on hand and a management plan in readiness. (For more on management, see below.)

Causes of anaphylaxis

There are many possible causes (or 'allergens') of anaphylactic reactions in susceptible children. The most common allergens are:

- *certain foods:* including nuts (especially peanuts), eggs, shellfish, and cow's milk;
- *certain medications:* including antibiotics (such as penicillin); and
- *stinging insects:* especially bees, wasps, and ants.

Signs and symptoms of anaphylaxis

There are several possible signs and symptoms of an anaphylactic reaction. The Box below lists these. However, because the reaction can come on very quickly, not every sign or symptom occurs in every case.

Management of anaphylaxis

If a child suffers an anaphylactic reaction, it is important to act quickly, but calmly.

An emergency ambulance should be called immediately. However, the child should never be left unattended; it is better to shout for help than leave the child alone.

Signs and symptoms of anaphylaxis

Signs and symptoms of an anaphylactic reaction include the following:

- generalised flushing of skin; itching; rash (hives/urticaria);
- facial swelling; tingling in or around mouth; metallic taste;
- increased heart rate; palpitations of the heart;
- abdominal cramps; nausea; vomiting; diarrhoea;
- sense of 'doom' (a feeling of impending death);
- cough or wheeze;
- swelling of throat and tongue; difficulty swallowing or breathing;
- loss of consciousness and/or collapse.

Note: The reaction can occur very quickly; not every sign or symptom occurs in every case.

Technical terms used in this chapter

This chapter uses some technical terms as a 'shorthand' way of describing what happens in emergencies. Most of these are explained in the text, but this list might also be helpful.

Adrenaline
A medication given by injection to reverse the effects of a severe allergic reaction; also called epinephrine (or 'epi')

Allergen
Something that sets off an allergic reaction—such as food, medications, or stings from insects

Anaphylaxis
A severe life-threatening allergic reaction

Cardiac arrest
The heart has stopped beating

Cardio-
To do with the heart

CPR
Cardiopulmonary resucitation (heart–lung resuscitation)

Incontinence of urine
Loss of ability to control the bladder

Pulmonary
To do with the lungs

Respiratory arrest
The breathing has stopped; the person has stopped inhaling and exhaling

Resuscitation
Techniques that attempt to 'revive' life by stimulating the heart and lungs

Seizure
A 'convulsion' or a 'fit'; usually refers to a sudden, involuntary contraction of the muscles of the body

Sign
Something that a parent or carer notices in a sick child (such as a rash)

Symptom
Something that the sick child complains about but other people cannot see (such as pain)

As noted above, every child who is known to have a potential anaphylactic reaction should have emergency medications on hand and a management plan in readiness. In particular, such children should have a pre-loaded syringe of adrenaline (also called 'epinephrine' or 'epi'). A child who might require treatment with one of these syringes should have it 'on hand' at all times. It is obviously useless to have the child in one place (for example, at school) and the pre-loaded syringe some distance away (for example, at home). It is also important to advise teachers and other carers of the risk of anaphylaxis, and to discuss the use of the pre-loaded syringe if required.

These pre-loaded syringes are designed for easy use by untrained people (including the child) without the assistance of a doctor or nurse. In essence, the cap is simply taken from the pre-loaded syringe and the needle is pushed against the thigh. The medication is then automatically injected. Parents and carers can obtain advice on the proper use of the syringe from the manufacturers or from various hospitals and medical clinics. Some hospitals or clinics supply visiting nurses to give expert advice.

Any attempt at resuscitation is better than none in a critical life-threatening situation.

Oxygen should be given if this is available. The ambulance will have oxygen when it arrives.

If breathing stops, attempts should be made to resuscitate the child. All parents and carers should, ideally, have basic training in CPR (cardiopulmonary resuscitation). However, even if they are not confident of their skills, parents and carers should still attempt resuscitation. Any attempt at resuscitation is better than none in a critical life-threatening situation. (For more on resuscitation, see this chapter, page 129.)

Any child who has an anaphylactic reaction should be admitted to hospital. Even after apparent recovery from an anaphylactic reaction, children can deteriorate again. This can occur up to 12 hours after the initial event.

Seizures

Seizures, fits, and convulsions

The terms 'seizure', 'fit', and 'convulsion' all mean the same thing. They all describe the same event—usually referring to a sudden, violent, involuntary contraction of the muscles of the body (although not all 'seizures' are like this, see below). The word 'seizure' is now considered to be the most appropriate term to use.

Types of seizures

Although the term 'seizure' usually refers to a generalised convulsion of the body, not all seizures involve such violent contractions of many muscles at once. In fact, a seizure can take many forms. These include the following.

- 'absence' seizures;
- myoclonic seizures;
- atonic seizures; and
- generalised seizures.

These are briefly described below.

'Absence' seizures

These involve a temporary lack of attention for a minute or so. The child appears to be 'somewhere else'. There is no muscle spasm and the child does not usually fall down or slump over; the child simply sits quietly and blankly (with perhaps some blinking of the eyes).

These seizures tend to occur more often in younger children of primary-school age. They can occur several times a day.

'Absence' seizures do not require any immediate treatment, but the child should be taken to a doctor for assessment when they first occur.

Myoclonic seizures

These seizures involve sudden spasms of a muscle or a small group of muscles—similar to the common jerking movement of an arm or a leg that most people have experienced as they go to sleep.

These seizures do not require treatment if they occur infrequently, but the child should be taken to a doctor for assessment if they occur more often.

Atonic seizures

These are sometimes called 'drop attacks'. They involve a sudden complete loss of muscle tone. The child simply drops to the floor—with or without a loss of consciousness. Injuries can occur as the child falls. Medical assessment is required.

Generalised seizures

These are the well-known seizures with loss of consciousness and generalised muscle contractions affecting the whole body.

The seizure usually begins with sudden spasm of the muscles. This produces rigidity of the body, and the child falls down. Jerking movements of the head, arms, and legs can occur.

The child usually loses consciousness and develops noisy breathing. There is often salivation from the mouth and incontinence of urine.

Most of these seizures last less than ten minutes. However, they can sometimes persist for longer than this. It is very unlikely that a seizure will cause any brain damage.

Management

Generalised seizure

The first-aid management of generalised seizures is summarised in the Box below. The text that follows provides more information.

First-aid treatment of generalised seizures

In caring for a child who is having a generalised seizure, the following steps should be taken. These are explained in more detail in the text.

- Keep calm.
- Protect child from injury.
- Do not restrain the child.
- Do not insert anything in the child's mouth.
- Roll child onto side (when jerking movements have ceased).
- Call ambulance if seizure continues.
- Talk gently to child.

Keep calm

Although a generalised seizure can be a frightening event to witness, parents and carers should keep calm. The child will not die, and no long-term consequences are likely to occur.

Protect from injury

The child should be protected from injury—especially from surrounding furniture. If the child is sitting or slumped, he or she should be gently eased to the floor. Any hard or sharp objects in the vicinity should be moved out of the way.

Without restraining the child in any way, parents and carers can use their own bodies to shield the child's head and body from injury. Any tight clothing should be loosened. A small pillow or padding can be placed under the head.

No restraint

The child should not be restrained in any way. No attempt should be made to grab the child's arms and legs—because this can, in itself, cause injury.

If the child is still conscious, any attempt at restraint can cause increased agitation. The child should be gently reassured and, if necessary, led away from danger.

Insert nothing in mouth

Do not attempt to insert anything in the child's mouth. Contrary to popular belief, the child *cannot* swallow his or her tongue.

Strong contractions of the jaw muscles are common in seizures. Any attempt to place fingers in the child's mouth is likely to result in the parent or carer being bitten. Attempts to place solid objects in the child's mouth are likely to result in the child's teeth being broken.

Contrary to popular belief, the child *cannot* swallow his or her tongue.

Roll onto side

After the seizure subsides, the child should be rolled onto his or her side. This allows saliva to flow from the mouth and ensures that this is not inhaled. If there is any vomit in the child's mouth after the seizure has subsided, this can now be removed with a finger.

Call ambulance

If the child is known to have had previous seizures, there is no immediate need to call an ambulance. However, an ambulance should be called if any of the features listed in the Box on page 129 are present.

Talk gently to child

After the seizure has subsided, parents and carers should talk gently to the child offering comfort and reassurance. The child might need help to become reoriented in place and time (knowing where he or she is, and knowing the time of day).

If the child wishes to sleep, he or she should be allowed to do so under observation. If the child 'wanders', parents and carers should stay with the child and continue to talk gently.

When to call an ambulance after a seizure

After a seizure has subsided, an ambulance should be called if:

- the seizure is the child's first OR the seizure does not follow the child's 'usual pattern';
- the seizure continues for more than 10 minutes;
- the child has repeated seizures without waking up;
- the seizure occurs in water (see below for more on managing seizures in water);
- the child appears to be injured; or
- the child does not regain consciousness.

Management in a wheelchair

If the child is in a wheelchair at the time of a seizure, the management is much the same as described above—except that the child is not removed from the wheelchair. Parents and carers should:

- ensure that the brakes are on;
- prevent the child from falling from the chair;
- support the child's head; and
- move or pad any objects (or parts of the wheelchair) that might cause injury.

Management in water

If the child is in water at the time of the seizure (for example, in a swimming pool), the most important thing is to ensure that the child is turned face up, and that the face is then supported out of the water. The child should then be gently moved to the shallow end of the pool with the head tilted back (to assist with breathing). The child should then be removed from the water as soon as possible. Care should be taken to ensure that the child is not injured in the process of getting out of the pool.

Once out of the water, the child should be laid on his or her side. The child's breathing should then be checked. If there is no breathing, CPR (cardiopulmonary resuscitation) should be started. (For more on CPR, see below.)

> The most important thing is to ensure that the child is turned face up, and that the face is then supported out of the water.

An ambulance should be called for any child who has a seizure in water. The child needs to be carefully assessed after the seizure has subsided.

Resuscitation

Importance of learning resuscitation

As this book has mentioned several times, every parent or carer should know basic first aid—including CPR (cardiopulmonary resuscitation). Most centres usually have first-aid courses available from time to time, and parents and carers should make every effort to attend these classes and learn these important CPR skills.

A book like this cannot replace a proper first-aid class, but some important points can be made that will be helpful in an emergency. Reading about these matters might also encourage untrained parents and carers to enrol in a first-aid course and learn the techniques themselves—especially if they find, after reading the rest of this chapter, that CPR is not all that difficult after all!

What is CPR?

The letters 'CPR' stand for cardiopulmonary resuscitation—or, in other words, 'heart–lung resuscitation'. As the name suggests, CPR consists of two important parts:

- *cardio:* heart resuscitation (to get the blood circulation going); and
- *pulmonary:* lung resuscitation (to get the breathing going).

In simple terms, the first is achieved by repeated pressing down in the centre of the lower chest to produce compression of the heart (so-called 'cardiac compression'). The second is achieved by mouth-to-mouth breathing ('mouth-to-mouth resuscitation').

Most people will have seen these two techniques used at some time—even if only on television dramas or in the movies! However, even this sort of limited experience of seeing CPR can be worthwhile for untrained parents and carers. As this book has noted several times: *any attempt at CPR is better than no attempt!* If an untrained parent or carer is confronted with a life-threatening situation, they should at least attempt CPR—even if their only experience of the techniques is what they have seen on television or what they read in this book. It would obviously be better if every parent and carer was properly trained in CPR techniques. But this is not an ideal world, and untrained parents and carers should always be prepared to at least *make an attempt* at CPR if this is required. It could save a child's life.

If an untrained parent or carer is confronted with a life-threatening situation, they should at least attempt CPR.

Difference between children and adults

In CPR, there is an important difference between children and adults that should be considered. The difference is that, in children, it is very rare for the heart to stop before the lungs. Putting this in technical terms, a child nearly always has a respiratory arrest *before* a cardiac arrest. An adult can have a sudden massive heart attack—and collapse immediately with both the heart and lungs not working. But a child will nearly always get into breathing difficulties *before* the heart stops beating.

This has two important implications.

- *It gives warning:* There will nearly always be a *warning* that a child is getting into severe difficulties. Parents and carers should therefore be alert for any signs that their child is having increasing problems with breathing or any signs that the child's colour is deteriorating—especially any signs that the child is going very pale or blue.
- *It shows the importance of mouth-to-mouth:* Because children nearly always have a respiratory arrest before a cardiac arrest, immediate mouth-to-mouth resuscitation will often save a child's life—without the need for cardiac compression. The *first thing* that should always be done in administering CPR to a child is to give two effective breaths by mouth-to-mouth breathing. This will often start the heart again. More detail on how

to do this is provided below, but the important thing to remember is that two effective breaths by immediate mouth-to-mouth breathing might well save the child's life without the need for further CPR.

Giving mouth-to-mouth

Basic technique for mouth-to-mouth

The basic technique for giving mouth-to-mouth is summarised in the Box below.

Basic technique for mouth-to-mouth

In giving mouth-to-mouth to children and adults, the basic technique is:

- have the person lying on his or her back;
- tilt the head back (only slightly in a child, but fully back in an adult);
- hold the person's nose closed;
- open the person's mouth a little;
- seal the person's mouth with your own mouth; and
- breathe firmly and fully into the person's open mouth until the chest rises; the breath should be given over about one second.

Note: In giving mouth-to-mouth to infants, cover the infant's mouth and nose with your mouth. If you cannot effectively cover the mouth and nose, close the infant's mouth and cover his or her nose with your mouth. Breathe gently until the chest rises.

Giving the two initial breaths

In giving the two initial breaths mentioned above (see page 130), it is important to know that the breaths in mouth-to-mouth should be 'controlled full breaths'. In other words, there is no value in giving quick 'panting' breaths in rapid succession.

It might seem difficult to remain calm and give 'controlled full breaths' in an emergency situation—and some parents and carers might even think that giving rapid breaths will be more effective. However, two 'proper' breaths provide more oxygen and give better inflation to the lungs than a series of quick, shallow breaths. The breaths from the parent or carer should last about one second each, and each one should make the child's chest rise.

Even if the parent or carer is feeling very anxious, it is important to remain calm and give two 'controlled full breaths' before doing anything else. This might well save the child's life.

The breaths in mouth-to-mouth should be "controlled full breaths".

Giving cardiac compression

Knowing whether to begin cardiac compression

If the two breaths by mouth-to-mouth do not get the child breathing again, it might be necessary to add cardiac compression.

The aim of cardiac compression is to get the blood circulating again. In theory, there is no need to do this if the heart is still beating—but this is sometimes difficult for untrained parents and carers to judge. They can try to feel for a pulse (if they know how to do this), but it is easy to make mistakes—especially in an emergency. People sometimes believe that they can feel a pulse—when there is actually *no pulse* present. Alternatively, they can sometimes 'miss' a pulse—when there actually *is* one present. It is not easy.

> The best advice is to give the two breaths and immediately start cardiac compressions—unless there is obvious sign of breathing.

The best advice is to give the two breaths and immediately start cardiac compressions—unless there is obvious sign of breathing. If the child's heart *is* actually still beating, cardiac compression will do no harm. However, if the child's heart is *not* beating, cardiac compression might save the child's life. If in doubt, do it!

Basic technique for cardiac compression

The basic technique for administering cardiac compression is summarised in the Box below.

Rates of breathing and compressing

When people are taught CPR in a proper first-aid course, they are taught the *exact* rates of compression and mouth-to-mouth breathing to use. In other words, they are taught how many compressions to administer for each mouth-to-mouth breath administered, and how rapidly to give these.

Basic technique for cardiac compression

The basic technique for administering cardiac compression is as follows.

Where?

Locate the position where the ribs meet at the top of the abdomen and the lower end of the chest. This is the position to push—on the bones at the bottom of the chest, not on the soft tummy.

Push with fingers or whole hand?

Push down firmly with the fingers or the hand as follows:

- For an infant, use two fingers of your hand.
- For a child, use the 'heel' of one or two of your hands.
- For an older child or adult, use the 'heels' of both your hands.

If in doubt whether to use the fingers or the whole hand, simply use whatever 'seems right' for the size of the child's chest.

How far to push?

Press down firmly enough to compress the lower chest by *one-third of the normal chest diameter for that child*.

How often?

Press down about 30 times for every two mouth-to mouth breaths. (For more detail on this, see the text, page 133.)

The recommended rate is 30 compressions (at a rate of 100 per minute) to every two breaths. However, this can be difficult to remember—especially for untrained parents and carers in an emergency. If in doubt, simply remember that people breathe much less often than their hearts beat. Parents and carers should therefore give a large number of compressions (quite quickly), and then a couple of breaths. They should repeat this about five times before stopping to check if there is any response.

Final words of advice

These brief notes on giving CPR are not meant to replace proper training in CPR. It is obviously best if parents and carers enrol in an accredited course, learn the techniques, and practise them regularly. However, these notes might encourage untrained parents and carers—especially those who are hesitant about the whole thing—to know that CPR is not all that difficult. It is hoped that they might now be inspired to do a first-aid course and get themselves properly trained.

Any attempt at CPR is better than no attempt!

However, if an emergency occurs before they have had an opportunity to do a proper course in CPR, untrained parents and carers should always remember that any attempt at CPR is better than no attempt!

abrasion a scraping or rubbing injury

acute recent, sudden, short-lived; (note that 'acute' does not necessarily mean 'severe'; rather, 'acute' refers to the *time-span* involved; it is the opposite of 'chronic')

adrenaline a medication given by injection to reverse the effects of a severe allergic reaction; also called epinephrine (or 'epi')

airways the tubes leading down to, and through, the lungs

allergen something in the environment (for example, pollen, food, medication) that triggers an allergic reaction in certain people

amnesia a loss of memory

amputation cutting-off of part of the body

analgesics pain-killers

anaphylactic reaction severe, life-threatening allergic reaction

antibiotics medications that kill bacteria

antihistamines medications that stop or decrease an allergic response

antiinflammatory a medication (tablet, cream, etc.) that reduces inflammation

appendicitis inflammation of the appendix

arthralgia painful joints

atopy/atopic condition allergic tendency (for example, hives, eczema, hayfever)

avulsion injury pulling-off or tearing-away of the skin and underlying tissues

bacteria micro-organisms (microbes) that reproduce by themselves and can be killed by antibiotics; they are different from viruses (which can reproduce only by taking over another living cell and forcing it to replicate viruses)

benign not dangerous; no long-term effects

bronchi large airways inside the lungs

bronchioles small airways inside the lungs

bronchiolitis inflammation of smaller airways; usually caused by a viral infection; seen especially in infants and small children

bronchitis inflammation of large airways in lungs; usually caused by viral or bacterial infection

bronchodilator an asthma medication that relaxes the airways and opens up the lungs; sometimes called 'reliever medication' (as opposed to 'preventive medication')

burn damage to skin (and perhaps underlying tissue) caused by dry heat; (as distinct from 'scalds', which are caused by moist heat)

cardiac arrest the heart has stopped beating

cardiac compression external pressure to the chest in an attempt to simulate the pumping action of the heart and get the blood circulating again

cardio- to do with the heart

cardiopulmonary resuscitation (CPR) heart–lung resuscitation; emergency resuscitation techniques used to simulate normal blood circulation and breathing

chemotherapy medications used to kill cancer cells

chronic long-term; the opposite of 'acute' (which means 'short-term')

circulation the blood supply to the body; the movement of blood around the body carrying oxygen and nutrients

clavicle the 'collarbone'—the prominent bone that runs from the centre of the chest to the shoulder.

coal tar skin treatments made from distillation of coal; used as an anti-inflammatory treatment for dermatitis

Colles fracture a fracture of the radius bone of the forearm, just above the wrist; usually with a typical 'dinner-fork' deformity.

concussion a temporary loss of brain function after a head injury

conditioner-and-comb method a recommended method for detecting and eliminating head lice

conjunctivitis inflammation of the membrane of the eyes

constipation having hard stools (faeces) that are difficult to pass; (note that 'constipation' does not refer to *how often* a child passes faeces, but *what the faeces are like*)

contusion a bruise

convulsion see **seizure**

cortisone medication (tablet, cream, etc.) that reduces inflammation; also called 'steroids'

CPR cardiopulmonary resuscitation (heart–lung resuscitation); emergency resuscitation techniques used to simulate normal blood circulation and breathing

croup a condition in which a small child's upper airways are constricted in response to an infection; characterised by a barking cough and a harsh noise (called a 'stridor') on breathing in

deformity wrong shape—especially a 'bent' fractured bone

dehydration lack of normal level of fluid in the body; commonly associated with vomiting and diarrhoea; can be serious (especially in very small children)

dental caries infected ('rotten') teeth and gums

dermatitis inflammation of the skin

dislocation a condition in which the bones of a joint are out of normal alignment; might or might not be associated with a fracture

displaced out of normal position (usually referring to a fractured bone end)

dizziness feeling 'faint' or 'light-headed'; 'dizziness' is thus different from 'vertigo' (which involves the sensation of things going round and round outside the head)

ectopic pregnancy a pregnancy occurring outside the uterus (womb)

encephalitis inflammation of the brain

epiglottitis a life-threatening infection of the epiglottis (a small flap-like structure in the throat)

epistaxis a nosebleed

erythema (or erythematous) the term 'erythema' simply means 'redness' (usually of the skin)

exhalation/exhaling breathing out

febrile having a fever

febrile convulsion a seizure associated with a fever

femur the long bone of the thigh

fit see **seizure**

fracture a break in a bone; contrary to popular belief, a 'fracture' and a 'break' are exactly the same thing

gastroenteritis inflammation of the stomach and intestines—caused by various microbes

humerus the long bone of the upper arm

hypersensitivity an 'over-reaction' to something in the environment

hypothalamus part of the brain that controls various basic bodily functions, including temperature

immunisation artificial protection against an infectious disease by giving a child an injection or oral preparation that stimulates the immune system to mount a defence against the infection in later life

immunity protected from infection as a result of previous exposure to that infection or immunisation against it

impetigo school sores; infection of the skin caused by bacteria; spread by scratching or picking at the sores

incontinence of urine loss of ability to control the bladder

incubation period the time from when a child gets an infection until he or she becomes unwell

inflammation an area of redness, heat, swelling, and pain; occurs in response to infection, irritation, or injury; originally described in Latin as 'rubor, calor, tumor, and dolor' ('redness, heat, swelling, and pain')

inhalation/inhaling breathing in.

insecticides chemicals used to kill insects (such as mites and lice); insecticides should be used strictly as directed (and as little as possible)

intussusception (pronounced 'in-ta-sus-sep-sh'-n') a condition in which one portion of the intestine is telescoped inside the next portion of bowel.

laceration a cut or tear

laxatives medications or additions to the diet to make bowel actions (faeces, stools) easier to pass

lower respiratory tract infections: infections in the lower part of the lungs.

lymph nodes collections of white blood cells for fighting infection; nodes occur in various parts of the body (including around the throat, in the groins, and in the abdomen); often mistakenly called 'glands'

macule a small, flat area (or 'spot') of discoloured skin (usually less than 5 mm in diameter)

maculo–papular a combination of small flat 'spots' and raised 'spots' on the skin; this sort of rash is typical of measles

management an overall plan of treatment and prevention

meningococcal disease a rare but dangerous infection of the brain and/or blood caused by bacteria; see also **petechiae**

microbe microscopic organisms that can cause disease (mainly bacteria or viruses)

musculoskeletal something affecting the muscles and bones of the body

mycoplasma a microorganism similar to bacteria that causes respiratory infections

nodule a larger swelling on the skin surface (usually more than 5 mm in diameter); it extends deep into skin, and is usually firm to the touch.

oral rehydration replacement of fluid by drinking through the mouth

otitis media middle ear infection

papule a small, raised area of skin (less than 5 mm); it usually has a domed top (although it can be flat)

patella the kneecap

pertussis whooping cough

petechiae (pronounced 'p-teek-ee-eye') small, flat, red-brown (or purplish) spots on the skin up to 2 mm in diameter; it is important to note that they do not blanch (turn white) when pressure is applied with a finger—in contrast to most rashes in children which *do* fade when pressure is applied; petechiae are caused by tiny spots of blood gathered under the surface of the skin; they are important in diagnosing meningococcal disease

photophobia dislike of the light

preventive medication medication that aims to prevent episodes of asthma occurring

prodrome the early signs and symptoms of an infectious illness before a rash appears; typical prodrome signs and symptoms include fever, runny, nose, and cough

pulmonary to do with the lungs

purpura areas of little **petechiae** joined together; these are therefore larger areas (usually more than 2 mm) of bleeding under the skin.

pustule a **vesicle** containing yellow fluid

radius one of the two long bones of the forearm.

raised intra-cranial pressure increased pressure on the brain inside the skull; usually caused by a brain tumour, abscess, or injury

recurrent something that comes back again

rehydration replacement of fluid to restore normal levels of fluid in the body

reliever medication also called a **bronchodilator**; a medication that relaxes the airways and opens up the lungs; a 'treatment' medication (as opposed to 'preventive' medication)

respiratory arrest the breathing has stopped; the person has stopped inhaling and exhaling

resuscitation techniques that attempt to 'revive' life by stimulating the heart and lungs

scald damage to skin (and perhaps underlying tissue) caused by moist heat—such as boiling water; (as distinct from 'burns', which are caused by dry heat)

secretory glands glands that put out fluid

seizure a 'convulsion' or a 'fit'; usually refers to a sudden, involuntary contraction of the muscles of the body with loss of consciousness

self-limiting something that goes away on its own.

septicaemia 'blood-poisoning'; a significant infection of the blood in which bacteria are actively multiplying in the blood

sign something that a parent or carer notices in a sick child (such as a rash); a 'sign' is thus different from a 'symptom' (which is something that the sick child complains about but other people cannot see—such as pain)

sprain an injury to a joint; a 'sprain' is different from a 'strain' (which is an injury to a muscle)

steroid medication (tablet, cream, etc.) that reduces inflammation; also called 'cortisone'

strain an injury to a muscle; a 'strain' is different from a 'sprain' (which is an injury to a joint)

stridor a loud noise that indicates obstruction to breathing; heard when a child is *inhaling* (breathing in); commonly occurs in croup

subarachnoid haemorrhage a serious haemorrhage (bleed) under one of the membranes covering the brain

susceptible people who are liable to get a disease for various reasons—because they have not had it before, or because they have not had an immunisation, or because they have some other medical problem

symptom something that the sick child complains about but other people cannot see (such as pain); a 'symptom' is thus different from a 'sign' (which is something that a parent or carer notices in a sick child—such as a rash)

symptomatic treatment treatment that aims to relieve symptoms (such as itch or pain) without attempting to cure the cause

syndrome a collection of signs and symptoms

tibia the main long bone of the lower leg

trauma injury caused by external force

undisplaced still in normal position (usually referring to a fractured bone end)

upper respiratory tract infections infections in the nose, throat, and upper airways (top part of the lungs)

urinary tract infection an infection of the urinary tract—especially the bladder and/or kidneys; often called a 'UTI'

urticaria 'hives'; an allergic skin reaction

vertigo things in the environment seeming to go 'round and round' outside the head; vertigo is thus different from 'dizziness' (which is someone feeling 'light-headed' or 'faint')

vesicle a skin spot with a fluid-filled centre; vesicles are typical of chickenpox rash and 'cold sores'

viruses micro-organisms (microbes) that can reproduce only by taking over another living cell and forcing it to replicate viruses; not killed by conventional antibiotics, but can be killed by special anti-viral medications; viruses are different from bacteria (which reproduce by themselves and *can* be killed by antibiotics)

wheeze a noise that indicates obstruction to breathing; heard when a child is *exhaling* (breathing out).

Index